# Pocket Genius

# EARTH

## FACTS AT YOUR FINGERTIPS

LONDON, NEW YORK, MUNICH,
MELBOURNE, and DELHI

**DK DELHI**
**Project editor** Rashmi Rajan
**Project art editor** Nishesh Batnagar
**Senior editor** Samira Sood
**Senior art editor** Govind Mittal
**Editor** Neha Chaudhary
**Art editor** Pooja Pipil
**DTP designers** Jaypal Singh, Arjinder Singh
**Picture researcher** Sumedha Chopra
**Managing editor** Saloni Talwar
**Managing art editor** Romi Chakraborty
**CTS manager** Balwant Singh
**Production manager** Pankaj Sharma

**DK LONDON**
**Senior editor** Fleur Star
**Senior art editor** Philip Letsu
**US editor** Margaret Parrish
**Jacket editor** Manisha Majithia
**Jacket designer** Laura Brim
**Jacket manager** Amanda Lunn
**Production editor** Adam Stoneham
**Production controller** Mary Slater

**Publisher** Andrew Macintyre
**Associate publishing director** Liz Wheeler
**Art director** Phil Ormerod
**Publishing director** Jonathan Metcalf

**Consultant** Douglas Palmer

**TALL TREE LTD.**
**Editors** Rob Colson, Joe Fullman, Jon Richards
**Designer** Ed Simkins

First published in the United States in 2012
by DK Publishing
375 Hudson Street, New York, New York 10014
Copyright © 2012 Dorling Kindersley Limited
12 13 14 15 16  10 9 8 7 6 5 4 3 2 1
001–184267–Oct/12

A catalog record for this book
is available from the Library of Congress.
ISBN: 978-0-7566-9815-7

Printed and bound by South China
Printing Company, China

**Discover more at**
**www.dk.com**

# CONTENTS

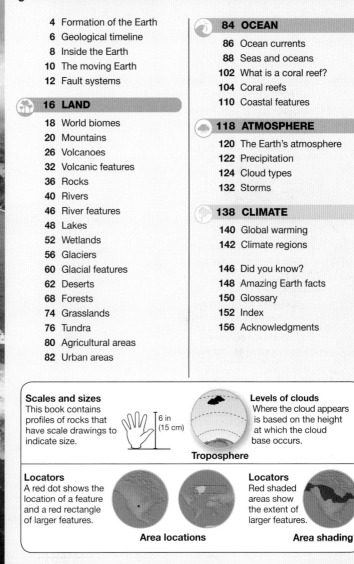

**Scales and sizes**
This book contains profiles of rocks that have scale drawings to indicate size.

6 in (15 cm)

**Levels of clouds**
Where the cloud appears is based on the height at which the cloud base occurs.

**Troposphere**

**Locators**
A red dot shows the location of a feature and a red rectangle of larger features.

**Area locations**

**Locators**
Red shaded areas show the extent of larger features.

**Area shading**

# Formation of the Earth

About 14 billion years ago, the universe was born in an incredibly violent explosion known as the Big Bang. In a fraction of a second, the speck-sized universe expanded into a huge fireball of gases. It cooled over time, forming stars, galaxies (large groups of stars), and planets, including the Earth.

The **solar system** formed from a spinning cloud of gas and dust

Particles in the disk clumped together to form **small bodies**

The center of the cloud heated up to form the **Sun,** with a spinning disk of gas and dust around it

## The birth of the Earth and the Moon

The young Earth was a red-hot ball of molten rock, or magma. Around 4.6 billion years ago, it was struck by a large body the size of the planet Mars. Vast amounts of debris were thrown into space, where they gathered together to form the Moon. Over time, the Earth cooled to become a rocky planet, with oceans, continents, and an atmosphere.

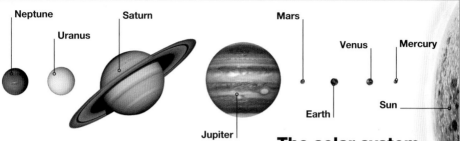

Neptune  Uranus  Saturn  Jupiter  Mars  Venus  Mercury  Sun  Earth

## The solar system

The solar system is made up of the Sun, eight planets, more than 170 moons, and millions of small, rocky bodies, such as asteroids and comets. The planets revolve around the Sun in paths called orbits. The four planets closest to the Sun are balls of rock and metal, while the other four are made up mostly of gas and liquid.

The small bodies crashed into each other and joined to create **planets**

**Formation of the solar system**

## GOLDILOCKS PLANET

**The Earth is the only planet** in our solar system that supports life. It is called a "Goldilocks planet," after the story of *Goldilocks and the Three Bears*. Just as Goldilocks found the porridge that was "just right" for her to eat, the Earth is "just right" to support life—neither too hot nor too cold, and with large amounts of liquid water, which allows life to flourish.

# Geological timeline

People who study the Earth are called geologists. Using sources such as fossils, rocks, and minerals, they have divided the Earth's history into different portions of time. The longest are called eons, which are made up of eras, which consist of periods.

## First life

About three billion years ago, the first traces of life appeared in the form of bacteria living in shallow seas. They built mounds out of sand, called stromatolites. These mounds are still forming in some areas today, and provide a record of life on the Earth.

**Stromatolites**

| PERIOD | | Cambrian | Ordovician | Silurian | Devonian | Carboniferous |
|---|---|---|---|---|---|---|
| ERA | | 542 million years ago (mya) | | PALEOZOIC ERA | | |
| EON | | PHANEROZOIC | | | | |

## Complex life

Life-forms grew much more complex during the Cambrian period. From Ordovician times onward, small land plants began to develop. By the Devonian period, bigger fernlike and treelike plants formed the first forests, along with giant fungi, such as *Prototaxites*. These provided habitats for the first land animals.

**About 7 in (18 cm) Aglaophyton are dwarfed by giant fungi**

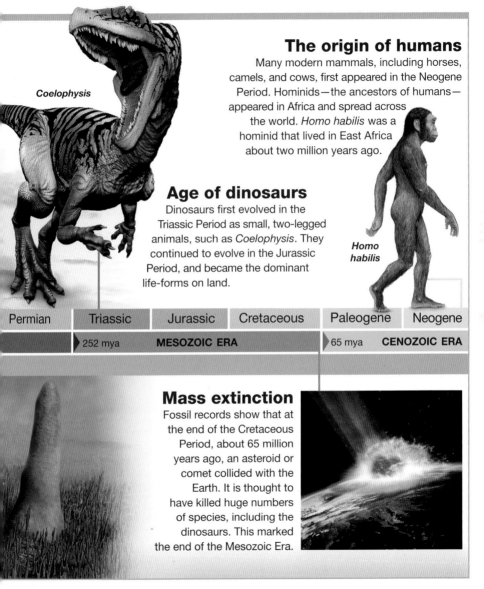

*Coelophysis*

# The origin of humans

Many modern mammals, including horses, camels, and cows, first appeared in the Neogene Period. Hominids—the ancestors of humans—appeared in Africa and spread across the world. *Homo habilis* was a hominid that lived in East Africa about two million years ago.

# Age of dinosaurs

Dinosaurs first evolved in the Triassic Period as small, two-legged animals, such as *Coelophysis*. They continued to evolve in the Jurassic Period, and became the dominant life-forms on land.

*Homo habilis*

| Permian | Triassic | Jurassic | Cretaceous | Paleogene | Neogene |
|---|---|---|---|---|---|
| | ▶ 252 mya | **MESOZOIC ERA** | | ▶ 65 mya | **CENOZOIC ERA** |

# Mass extinction

Fossil records show that at the end of the Cretaceous Period, about 65 million years ago, an asteroid or comet collided with the Earth. It is thought to have killed huge numbers of species, including the dinosaurs. This marked the end of the Mesozoic Era.

# Inside the Earth

The inside of the Earth has three main layers: a thin, cool outer crust; a thick, hot mantle; and an even hotter metallic core. The movement of heat from the core through the mantle has caused the rocks of the Earth's crust to change over time.

The Earth **bulges** at the equator

**Inner core** is 1,700 miles (2,740 km) thick

Direction of the **Earth's rotation**

## Shape and form

The force of gravity pulls the Earth into an almost perfect sphere. However, the Earth rotates on its axis, which causes it to bulge slightly at the equator.

## The Earth's layers

The Earth's outermost layer is the crust, which is made of soil and rock. Under this is the mantle, where liquid rock, or magma, flows in huge swirls. However, the inside, or core, of the Earth has two sections—an outer core of thick liquid rock, and a solid inner core.

**Layers of the Earth**

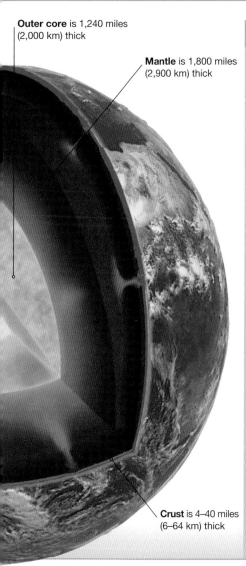

**Outer core** is 1,240 miles (2,000 km) thick

**Mantle** is 1,800 miles (2,900 km) thick

**Crust** is 4–40 miles (6–64 km) thick

## TYPES OF ROCK

**Igneous rocks** form from molten rock that has cooled and turned solid. They originate from deep inside the Earth, and may form at or below the Earth's surface.

**Sedimentary rocks** form at the Earth's surface and are made up of clearly visible layers of minerals, rock pieces, or organic matter (such as the remains of animals and plants).

**Metamorphic rocks**, such as this quartzite rock, form when existing rocks are squeezed by pressure and heated deep under the Earth's crust.

# The moving Earth

The Earth's crust is broken up into huge, irregularly shaped pieces called tectonic plates. These plates are pushed around by the movement of magma in the mantle below. This movement causes the Earth to change gradually, over millions of years—continents have been created, oceans have opened and closed, and mountains have risen.

## Plate tectonics

More than 200 million years ago, the Earth consisted of one large landmass—a "supercontinent" called Pangaea. The movement of the Earth's tectonic plates over millions of years broke up this landmass, creating the modern continents. This movement of plates is known as plate tectonics, and continues to take place today.

**270 million years ago**

**200 million years ago**

**Today**

## The Earth's plates

There are 30 tectonic plates, of which seven cover 94 percent of the Earth. The rest is made up of 23 smaller plates. The boundaries, or edges, of tectonic plates are usually marked by mountains, earthquake and volcanic zones, and oceanic trenches.

**The Earth's tectonic plates**

# Plate boundary

Where two tectonic plates meet, different types of plate boundary are formed, based on how the plates move. Plate movement can cause earthquakes and volcanic eruptions.

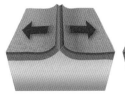

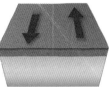

Where plates crash into each other, a **convergent boundary** occurs. Here, one plate may be pushed beneath the other in a process called subduction.

A **divergent boundary** is created where plates move away from each other. Molten lava may rise up from the mantle to fill the gap at this type of boundary.

Where two plates scrape past each other, a **transform boundary** occurs.

**Key**
▲ *Volcanic zone*
● *Hotspot*
● *Earthquake zone*
▬▬ *Pacific Ring of Fire*

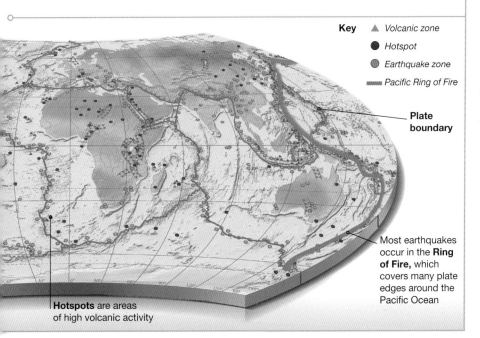

**Plate boundary**

Most earthquakes occur in the **Ring of Fire,** which covers many plate edges around the Pacific Ocean

**Hotspots** are areas of high volcanic activity

# Fault systems

The constant movement of the Earth's tectonic plates causes its crust to split apart. This can lead to massive blocks of rock slipping past one another, resulting in huge cracks in the Earth's surface called faults. Plates sometimes get stuck as they push past each other, causing energy to build up. When they eventually slip free, the sudden jolt can cause an earthquake.

## San Andreas Fault

The San Andreas Fault slices across California's coastal region. To its west is the Pacific plate, which stretches from the edge of California almost to Asia. To the east is the North American plate, which makes up most of the continent. The inhabited areas on this fault, particularly in southern California, are prone to earthquakes.

**LOCATION** From Cape Mendocino, northern California, to the Gulf of California

**PLATE BOUNDARY TYPE** Transform

**LENGTH** 808 miles (1,300 km)

Over the last century, the San Andreas Fault has been moving at an average rate of 2 in (5 cm) every year.

## Great Rift Valley

Africa's Great Rift Valley runs through the middle of Kenya. It is part of a huge set of cracks in the Earth's crust called the East African Rift System. In northeastern Africa, this system divides the African plate from the Arabian plate, cutting past the Sinai Peninsula.

**LOCATION**   From the southern Red Sea, through East Africa, to Beira in Mozambique

**PLATE BOUNDARY TYPE**   Divergent

**LENGTH**   4,000 miles (6,400 km)

*Sinai Peninsula*

## Sunda Megathrust

This fault lay inactive for a thousand years. But in 2004, a part of it slipped, causing a huge earthquake and tsunami in the Indian Ocean. Giant waves swept far inland, destroying coastlines and killing about 280,000 people.

**LOCATION**   From Bangladesh, through Sumatra, Bali, and Indonesia, to northwestern Australia

**PLATE BOUNDARY TYPE**   Convergent

**LENGTH**   3,400 miles (5,500 km)

## Great Alpine Fault

About 26 million years ago, the movement of the Pacific and Australian plates formed the Great Alpine Fault. Plate movement pushed the land up, creating the Southern Alps.

**LOCATION**   New Zealand's South Island west coast from Fiordland to Blenheim

**PLATE BOUNDARY TYPE**   Transform

**LENGTH**   300 miles (500 km)

# Half a million years ago, these crystals were as small as a grain of salt, but now they weigh

# 55 tons

## CAVE OF CRYSTALS
Giant crystals of selenite, a form of the mineral gypsum, are found 1,000 ft (300 m) below the Naica mine in Mexico. They formed when a magma chamber boiled the water below the Earth's surface at a consistent temperature for 500,000 years. The heat solidified the crystals in the water and helped them grow. They are now some of the largest natural crystals in the world.

# Land

About 30 percent of the Earth's surface is covered by land. A wide range of landscapes are found on the Earth, including mountains, deserts, forests, and grasslands. Many of these landscapes are shaped by the wind and rain, while others, such as deltas and valleys, are formed by rivers and glaciers. Human activity can also shape the landscape. People use the countryside as farmland to grow crops or herd animals, while urban areas feature tall buildings and well-developed roads and highways.

**VOLCANIC EFFECT**
Volcanic eruptions can change the landscape in many ways. When lava comes into contact with water, it can cool to form islands. Also, volcanic ash acts as fertilizer, helping plants grow.

# World biomes

Regions that share the same climate, soils, vegetation, and animals are known as biomes. Scientists divide the world into a number of biomes, or habitats, ranging from dry deserts with very little life to wet rainforests teeming with plants and animals.

**Tundra** regions are too cold for most trees to grow. The plant life mainly consists of tough grasses, mosses, and small shrubs.

**NORTH AMERICA**

There are two kinds of **grassland**: temperate, found in cool areas; and tropical, found in hot areas near the equator.

**SOUTH AMERICA**

**KEY**

- Polar regions
- Mountains
- Rainforests
- Coniferous forests
- Temperate forests
- Wetlands
- Grasslands
- Tundra
- Deserts
- Oceans

**Mountains** are high, rocky areas that are colder than most lower areas. Many mountains are permanently covered in ice and snow.

**Wetlands** are waterlogged or flooded areas of land. They may have salty or fresh water, and include mangroves, bogs, marshes, and fens.

Antarctica and the Arctic form the **polar regions,** which are the Earth's coldest zones. Polar regions cover about 20 percent of the Earth's surface.

**Coniferous forests** form the world's largest continuous land biome. They consist of coniferous trees that cover about 17 percent of the Earth's land area.

**EUROPE**

**ASIA**

**AFRICA**

**EQUATOR**

The largest biome on the Earth, **oceans** support a huge range of living species, from tiny plankton to the biggest animal in the world—the blue whale.

**AUSTRALIA**

**Rainforests** are found in regions with very wet climates. Tropical rainforests contain more plant and animal life than any other biome on the Earth.

**Temperate forests** lie roughly midway between the poles and the equator. They have distinct warm and cold seasons called summer and winter.

**Deserts** cover about one-fifth of the Earth's land surface. They receive little or no rain and very few animals and plants live in them.

**ANTARCTICA**

Many plants
and animals have
adapted to the cold
temperatures of
the mountains.

▲ Lady Amherst's
pheasant lives in the
mountain forests of
Asia. It moves up and
down the mountains
with the seasons.

▲ The dark color of the
Bhutan glory helps it to
absorb sunlight and warm
up quickly in the cold.

▲ The small, tough
leaves of alpine plants
reduce water loss and
protect them from very
cold temperatures.

# Mountains

Masses of rock that rise high above their
surroundings are called mountains. They
are pushed up by plate movements over
many millions of years to create soaring
peaks. At present, mountains cover
20 percent of the Earth's land surface.

### Rocky Mountains

The Rocky Mountains are made up of at least 100
separate ranges. They are part of one of the largest mountain
belts on Earth—the Western Cordillera. The landscape of the
mountain chain is complex and varied, with towering peaks
and active volcanoes.

**LOCATION** Western North America, from Alaska
to New Mexico

**HIGHEST PEAK** Mount McKinley, Alaska (20,321 ft/6,194 m)

**LENGTH** 3,700 miles (6,000 km)

## Andes

The Andes is the longest mountain chain in the world. Its peaks rise suddenly from sea level on the Pacific coast of South America to altitudes of over 21,500 ft (6,500 m). It is one of the Earth's most active mountain belts. There are frequent earthquakes as well as eruptions from 183 active volcanoes.

*Mount Fitzroy in Patagonia, southern Andes*

**LOCATION**  Down western South America, from the Caribbean Sea to Cape Horn

**HIGHEST PEAK**
Aconcagua, Argentina
(22,835 ft/6,960 m)

**LENGTH**
(4,500 miles/7,200 km)

## Urals

Also known as "the stone belt," the Ural mountain range separates Europe from Asia. The central and southern parts of this range are covered with thick forests, while farther north, there are alpine meadows and tundra.

**LOCATION**  From the Arctic Ocean to the border between Russia and Kazakhstan

**HIGHEST PEAK**  Narodnaya, Russia
(6,215 ft/1,895 m)

**LENGTH**  1,500 miles (2,400 km)

## Pyrenees

During the Cretaceous Period, Iberia split from the supercontinent of Pangaea. As the Atlantic Ocean opened, the Iberian plate was squeezed between Europe and North Africa, forming the Pyrenees. This range has some of Europe's most spectacular waterfalls and many limestone caves with paintings by early modern humans.

**LOCATION**  Between France and Spain, from the Atlantic Ocean to the Mediterranean Sea

**HIGHEST PEAK**  Aneto, Spain (11,170 ft/3,405 m)

**LENGTH**  270 miles (435 km)

## Alps

The Alps were created when the African and Eurasian plates collided around 90 million years ago. These mountains form a curved belt, with many peaks rising to above 13,000 ft (4,000 m). They form the largest mountain range in Europe.

## Atlas Mountains

These mountains do not form a continuous chain, but a series of different ranges. The northern ranges get plenty of rainfall and feature cedar, pine, and oak forests. The southern ranges are drier and have salt flats in areas close to the Sahara.

**LOCATION**  Across southern Europe,
from Mediterranean France to Austria

**HIGHEST PEAK**  Mont Blanc, France
(15,770 ft/4,805 m)

**LENGTH**  650 miles (1,050 km)

**LOCATION**  From the Atlantic coast
of Morocco to the Mediterranean east
coast of Tunisia

**HIGHEST PEAK**  Toubkal, Morocco
(13,665 ft/4,165 m)

**LENGTH**  1,500 miles (2,400 km)

## Drakensberg Plateau

Although the Drakensberg Plateau is
made up of sedimentary rocks, it is covered with
a layer of basalt, an igneous rock. This layer was
originally 4,900 ft (1,500 m) thick and covered an
area of about 800,000 sq miles (2 million sq km),
but over time, much has been worn away. The
plateau has steep sandstone cliffs, individual
pinnacles, waterfalls, and huge caves.

**LOCATION**  From northeastern to southern
South Africa, through Swaziland and Lesotho

**HIGHEST PEAK**  Ntlenyana, Lesotho
(11,417 ft/3,480 m)

**LENGTH**  800 miles (1,290 km)

# Himalayas

Formed within the last 50 million years, the Himalayas are one of the world's youngest mountain belts. They are the highest mountains on the Earth, and are getting higher at a rate of $\frac{1}{6}$ in (4 mm) every year, because the Indian plate is still pushing into the Eurasian plate.

**LOCATION**   From northern Pakistan and India, across Nepal to Bhutan

**HIGHEST PEAK**   Mount Everest, Nepal (29,035 ft/8,850 m)

**LENGTH**   2,400 miles (3,800 km)

# Great Dividing Range

This range is one of Australia's most important geographical features, since it is the source of many of the country's major rivers, including the Murray and the Darling. It runs along the length of Australia's eastern coast, with the highest peaks in the south.

**LOCATION**   From the Cape York Peninsula, Queensland, along Australia's eastern coast to Tasmania

**HIGHEST PEAK**
Mount Kosciuszko, Australia (7,310 ft/2,230 m)

**LENGTH**   2,237 miles (3,600 km)

## Southern Alps

New Zealand's Alps were formed by the collision of the Pacific plate and the Australian plate. The range is at its highest near the center. Its western slopes are covered in forests because of the year-round rains brought by the winds blowing from that direction.

**LOCATION** New Zealand's South Island, from northeast to southwest

**HIGHEST PEAK** Mount Cook, New Zealand (12,285 ft/3,745 m)

**LENGTH** 300 miles (500 km)

## Transantarctic Mountains

The curved belt of the Transantarctic Mountains separates the higher region of Greater Antarctica in the east from the lower Lesser Antarctica in the west. This belt includes many volcanoes, some of which are still active, such as Deception Island.

**LOCATION** Across Antarctica, from Oates Land to the Antarctic Peninsula

**HIGHEST PEAK** Vinson Massif, Antarctica (16,065 ft/4,895 m)

**LENGTH** 2,200 miles (3,500 km)

# Volcanoes

A volcano is both an opening in the Earth's crust through which magma, ash, and hot gases erupt from below its surface, and the structure created by this eruption. Volcanic eruptions can cause widespread destruction.

FOCUS ON...
## TYPES
There are many different types of volcano, depending on their shape or the way they were formed.

## Crater Lake

About 7,000 years ago, a massive eruption destroyed Mount Mazama and formed a crater, or caldera. Over time, heavy rain and snowfall caused water levels in the crater to rise, creating Crater Lake. As the lake is not fed by streams or rivers, which carry sediments—particles of rock, mineral, or plant and animal remains—its water is extremely clear.

**LOCATION**  Southern Cascade Range, Oregon
**TYPE**  Collapsed stratovolcano
**HEIGHT**  8,170 ft (2,490 m)

## Kilauea

Kilauea is the most active of the overlapping volcanoes that have built up the island of Hawaii, which rises more than 13,000 ft (4,000 m) from the ocean floor. Since 1983, flows from Kilauea have covered more than 40 sq miles (100 sq km).

**LOCATION**  Southeast Hawaii
**TYPE**  Shield volcano
**HEIGHT**  4,000 ft (1,220 m)

▲ A stratovolcano is cone-shaped, with steep slopes. It is built of many layers of lava and ash.

▲ A shield volcano is formed when runny basalt lava flows across the ground. It is usually broad, with shallow slopes.

▲ A submarine volcano forms deep under water and its eruption may or may not reach sea level.

## Surtsey

In November 1963, a series of volcanic explosions occurred off the coast of southern Iceland. When the smoke cleared, a new island had appeared above the waves. The Icelandic government named it Surtsey, after Surtur, a mythical Norse fire giant. The island continued to emit clouds of ash and fountains of lava until 1967, when it finally fell quiet.

| | |
|---|---|
| **LOCATION** | Off the coast of Iceland |
| **TYPE** | Submarine |
| **HEIGHT** | 500 ft (150 m) above sea level |

## Mount Etna

Europe's highest active volcano, Etna is almost constantly erupting. It produces rivers of basaltic lava that flow down to the foot of the volcano on all sides.

| | |
|---|---|
| **LOCATION** | Eastern Sicily, southwest Italy |
| **TYPE** | Stratovolcano |
| **HEIGHT** | 10,990 ft (3,350 m) |

## Mount Kilimanjaro

Rising from the savanna plains of eastern Africa, Kilimanjaro is the highest mountain on the continent. It is made up of three volcanic cones—Kibo, Mawenzi, and Shira—of which the central snow-capped cone, Kibo, is the highest.

**LOCATION** Southern end of the Great Rift Valley, northeastern Tanzania

**TYPE** Stratovolcano

**HEIGHT** 19,340 ft (5,895 m)

## Mount Fuji

Japan's highest mountain, Mount Fuji began to grow over 11,000 years ago on top of the remains of an older volcano. Within just 3,000 years, lava pouring out of its crater had built up 80 percent of its present mass.

**LOCATION** Honshu Island, southwest Tokyo

**TYPE** Stratovolcano

**HEIGHT** 12,390 ft (3,775 m)

## Mount Erebus

Glacier-covered Erebus is the southernmost active volcano on the Earth, and is one of three major volcanoes on Antarctica's Ross Island. Unusually, the crater at the top of Mount Erebus is permanently filled with molten lava.

**LOCATION** Ross Island, off the Scott Coast

**TYPE** Stratovolcano

**HEIGHT** 12,450 ft (3,795 m)

In 1991, the eruption of Mount Pinatubo

**lowered the Earth's temperatures**

by 1°F (0.5°C) for a year

**VOLCANIC ASH CLOUD**
Dust and ash can rain down for days after a volcanic eruption. The ash enters the atmosphere and blocks sunlight, affecting the weather. The 1991 eruption of Mount Pinatubo, in the Philippines, covered the surrounding region in a thick layer of ash.

# Volcanic features

When magma cools and solidifies under the Earth's surface, it creates a variety of features in different ways. Some are formed from igneous rock, some from water heated up by magma, and others from collapsed craters.

FOCUS ON...
## LAVA
Magma that has erupted onto the Earth's surface is called lava. It can take various forms after it cools.

## Yellowstone Caldera

This huge volcanic caldera is 45 miles (72 km) wide. It contains about 200 geysers—springs that release bursts of hot water and steam. It also has thousands of fumaroles (volcanic outlets that emit steam and other gases), boiling mud pools, and hot springs producing a steady stream of hot water.

**LOCATION** Yellowstone National Park, Wyoming

**TYPE** Geyser, hot spring, and fumarole

**AGE** 600,000 years

▲ Pahoehoe is a fast and smooth flowing hot lava. On cooling, it forms a wrinkled, ropelike skin.

▲ Aa is a basaltic lava that is thicker, stickier, and slower-flowing than pahoehoe. It forms a rough surface when it cools.

▲ Pillow lava is a pillow-shaped rock formed when lava erupts under water or comes in contact with water.

## Devil's Tower

Devil's Tower is a volcanic plug—a core of solidified magma blocking the neck of a volcano. Over millions of years, the surrounding sedimentary rocks wore away, leaving behind a tall, towerlike structure of igneous rock.

**LOCATION**  Great Plains of Wyoming

**TYPE**  Plug

**AGE**  40 million years

## Valley of Ten Thousand Smokes

In 1912, Novarupta Volcano erupted, filling the Ukak valley with ash. The water below the volcanic material heated up and worked its way up to the surface. For the next 15 years, snakelike wisps of steam escaped through thousands of cracks, which gave this valley its name.

**LOCATION**  Alaskan Peninsula

**TYPE**  Fumarole

**AGE**  100 years

## El Capitan and Half Dome

Batholiths are huge masses of igneous rock, which often form the core of mountains. Yosemite Valley, in the Sierra Nevada batholith, features huge, steep vertical cliffs and walls of granite. El Capitan, Yosemite's highest rock wall, rises more than 3,000 ft (900 m) above the valley floor. The area's steepest wall, Half Dome, was formed when a large glacier eroded away one side of the dome.

**LOCATION** Yosemite National Park, Sierra Nevada, California

**TYPE** Batholith

**AGE** 82 million years

## Giant's Causeway

This vent was formed as a result of intense volcanic activity about 60 million years ago. The eruption threw out large quantities of liquid basalt lava, which cooled to form about 40,000 hexagonal columns along the sea coast.

**LOCATION** Northernmost point of County Antrim, Northern Ireland, UK

**TYPE** Fissure vent

**AGE** 50–60 million years

## Aïr Mountains

The Aïr Mountains were created by volcanic eruptions after three continental plates collided. They are made up of ring dikes—circular sets of igneous intrusions formed around a volcano. Each set of rings is about 40 miles (60 km) in diameter, and contains dikes up to 650 ft (200 m) thick.

## Whin Sill

An igneous intrusion is created when magma enters cracks in existing rock. Often, it cools into a flat layer called a sill. Whin Sill is a collection of such sills, formed when magma rose from beneath the Earth's crust and spread. The name "whin" is a local word for hard, black stone.

**LOCATION**  Northern Pennine hills, England
**TYPE**  Sill
**AGE**  295 million years

**LOCATION**  Northern parts of Niger, Africa, within the southern Sahara Desert
**TYPE**  Ring dike
**AGE**  410 million years

# Rocks

Rocks are solid materials—consisting of one or more minerals—that make up the Earth's crust. Based on how they are formed, rocks can be classified into three main types—igneous, which form when magma becomes solid; sedimentary, which form when rock pieces or organic matter get deposited; and metamorphic, which form when there is a change in temperature or pressure.

## Granite

This rock is formed when magma cools slowly deep in the Earth's crust. Its toughness and resistance to erosion (wearing away) make it a popular choice for constructing roads and buildings.

**TYPE**  Igneous

**FORMATION**  Intense heat

**MINERALS**  Potassium-feldspar, quartz, sodium, and mica

**COLOR**  White-red, pale green-blue, and gray-black

## Basalt

The most common volcanic igneous rock on the Earth's surface, basalt forms the rock floor of most of the world's oceans. It is also found in large amounts on the Moon.

**TYPE**  Igneous

**FORMATION**  Intense heat

**MINERALS**  Sodium plagioclase, pyroxene, and olivine

**COLOR**  Grayish black to black when fresh

## Schist

Schist originates deep within mountain ranges. It usually has a medium to coarse texture, with visible mineral grains. It is rich in minerals such as mica and quartz.

**TYPE** Metamorphic
**FORMATION** High pressure and temperature
**MINERALS** Quartz, mica, and feldspar
**COLOR** Variable, including white and shades of gray, green, blue, brown, and black

## Slate

Slate is mud that has been heavily compressed, or packed together by pressure. Because of this compression, it is hard and waterproof, and can be split into thin sheets—all of which make it ideal for covering roofs.

**TYPE** Metamorphic
**FORMATION** Pressure
**MINERALS** Quartz, mica, and feldspar
**COLOR** Gray, also tinged green or purple

## Marble

Marble is valued for its smooth texture and color. It is easy to use in sculpture and construction. Pure marble is white, but some types have colorful patterns due to the presence of various minerals in them.

**TYPE** Metamorphic
**FORMATION** Heat and pressure
**MINERALS** Calcite
**COLOR** Mainly white, pink, green, brown, and black

## Limestone

This rock is made of the mineral calcite, which comes from sea water or the shells and skeletons of sea animals. On burning, it reduces lime, a mineral that is used to make cement.

**TYPE** Sedimentary

**FORMATION** Surface water deposition

**MINERALS** Calcite

**COLOR** Variable, but mostly white or pale shades of yellow, gray, or brown

## Sandstone

Sandstones are common rocks formed by deposits from air or water. Different types of sandstone form when minerals or rock grains the size of sand particles get stuck together. Sandstones are classified based on their texture.

**TYPE** Sedimentary

**FORMATION** Surface deposition

**MINERALS** Quartz and feldspar

**COLOR** Variable, including white, yellow, brown, to red-black

## Conglomerate

When larger rock debris is pressed together, it forms conglomerates. These may be made up of small pebbles, medium-sized cobbles, or large boulders. These rocks rarely contain fossils, because of their coarse nature and the tough conditions in which they are formed.

**TYPE** Sedimentary

**FORMATION** Surface water compression

**MINERALS** Calcite

**COLOR** Mainly white, pink, green, brown, and black

## Coal

This organic rock is made from the compressed remains of plants that existed millions of years ago. An important source of energy, coal is used to heat homes and generate electricity.

**TYPE** Sedimentary

**FORMATION** Compressed plant debris

**MINERALS** Clay

**COLOR** Black

## Evaporites

When hot, mineral-rich, salty water evaporates, it leaves behind minerals, such as halite (rock salt) and gypsum. Rocks made of these minerals are called evaporites. The crystal-like texture of these rocks is caused by the formation of salt crystals during evaporation. Many evaporites are used in the production of fertilizers and explosives.

*Crystal-like structure*

**TYPE** Sedimentary

**FORMATION** Surface evaporation of salty water

**MINERALS** Halite and gypsum

**COLOR** Usually white or pale shades of yellow and gray, through to red

# Rivers

A river is a channel of water that flows toward an ocean, lake, or sea. Smaller streams of water that flow into a river are known as its tributaries. Rivers are a powerful erosive force and they can wear down mountains, carve out valleys, and create wide flood plains.

## Mississippi

Along with its tributaries, the Mississippi forms a huge river system, which covers almost all of the US. Levees, or floodbanks, have been built along this river for protection against floods.

**LOCATION** US, from Canadian border in Minnesota to Gulf of Mexico

**LENGTH** 2,350 miles (3,780 km)

**TRIBUTARIES** Missouri, Ohio, Arkansas, and Tennessee

## Amazon

In terms of both the size of its basin (hollow depression) and the volume of water it carries, the Amazon is the largest river on the Earth. Its slow-moving stretches are covered with plants, such as giant water lilies, the leaves of which can grow up to about 6½ ft (2 m) wide.

**LOCATION**  Peruvian Andes, across Brazil to the Atlantic Ocean

**LENGTH**  3,995 miles (6,430 km)

**TRIBUTARIES**  Jurua, Madeira, and Negro

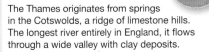

## Thames

The Thames originates from springs in the Cotswolds, a ridge of limestone hills. The longest river entirely in England, it flows through a wide valley with clay deposits.

**LOCATION**  Britain, across southern England from the Cotswold Hills to the North Sea

**LENGTH**  210 miles (335 km)

**TRIBUTARIES**  Colne, Kennet, and Wey

## Danube

The Danube begins at the meeting point of the Brege and Brigach rivers. The river also features the Iron Gate—the deepest gorge in Europe, with sides 2,625 ft (800 m) high.

**LOCATION**  Southern Germany to the Black Sea coast in eastern Romania

**LENGTH**  1,780 miles (2,860 km)

**TRIBUTARIES**  Drava, Sava, and Tisza

# Nile

The Nile is the longest river in the world. It is a valuable source of water for the region and has produced rich farmland along its banks. In the winter, rains and snowmelt from the Ethiopian mountains would cause the Nile to flood, depositing fertile soil across the flood plain. However, the construction of the Aswan High Dam in 1970 controlled this annual flooding and farmers now have to use artificial fertilizers.

**LOCATION**   From Lake Victoria and the Ethiopian Highlands through to the Mediterranean coast

**LENGTH**   4,130 miles (6,650 km)

**TRIBUTARIES**   White Nile, Blue Nile, and Atbara

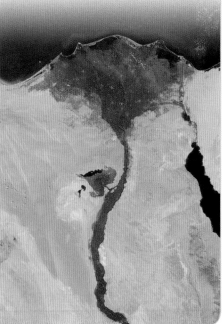

# Congo

The Congo is an important source of food and transportation to the people who live along its banks, but they live with the risk of flooding. Its flow is so strong and constant that it does not form a delta (a deposition of sediments at a river's mouth). Instead, it flows far out into the Atlantic Ocean, depositing sediments on the ocean floor.

# Indus

Like the Nile, the Indus was one of the rivers alongside which the first civilizations were founded. This river floods frequently in the summer, which can be dangerous for people who live along its banks.

**LOCATION** From east Africa, across the continent to the Atlantic Ocean

**LENGTH** 2,900 miles (4,670 km)

**TRIBUTARIES** Kwa, Lualaba, Sangha, and Ubangi

## Ganges

One of the most sacred rivers in India, the Ganges is worshiped as a goddess by Hindus. It carries more sand and silt to the sea than any other river in the world.

**LOCATION** Along the Himalayas to the Bay of Bengal in India

**LENGTH** 1,555 miles (2,505 km)

**TRIBUTARIES** Brahmaputra, Ghaghar, and Yamuna

**LOCATION** Tibetan Plateau, across the Himalayas to the Arabian Sea

**LENGTH** 1,800 miles (2,900 km)

**TRIBUTARIES** Chenab, Kabul, Jhelum, and Sutlej

## Murray

The water of the Murray is so salty that it cannot be used for anything except irrigation and power generation.

**LOCATION** Australia, from the Great Dividing Range to the Indian Ocean

**LENGTH** 1,610 miles (2,590 km)

**TRIBUTARIES** Darling and Murrumbidgee

In 1931, the Yangtze River flooded the cities of Nanjing and Wuhan, killing about 300,000 people and leaving

# 40 million homeless

**THE WALLED RIVER**
In the last 2,000 years, the Yangtze River in China has flooded at least 100 times, causing major destruction. To protect the surrounding areas from flooding, the banks of the Yangtze have been raised and dams have been built along its length.

# River features

As a river flows, it carves through the landscape or deposits sediments, creating various features along the way, such as waterfalls and deltas. Rivers can also dissolve rocks, creating karst landscapes with underground caves and passages.

## Carlsbad Cavern

Inside Carlsbad Caverns National Park, there are 110 limestone caves, including Carlsbad. This cavern has huge stalactites and stalagmites made of calcium and other minerals. The Big Room, formed about four million years ago, is its largest chamber, with an area of 357,480 sq ft (33,210 sq m).

**LOCATION**  Guadalupe Mountains of southern New Mexico
**TYPE**  Underground cave
**RIVER**  Pecos

## Niagara Falls

The Niagara Falls are the second largest waterfall in the world, and include the Bridal Veil, American, and Horseshoe falls. Originally, 5¹/₂ billion gallons (20 billion liters) of water flowed over the falls every hour. Today, dams and tunnels have been built to control the flow.

**LOCATION**  Border between Canada and US
**TYPE**  Waterfall
**RIVER**  Niagara

## Vercors

### Okavango Delta

The Okavango River starts in Angola and ends in a huge inland delta called the Okavango Delta. The river water pours into the delta, creating plant-rich wetlands that remain swampy throughout the year.

**LOCATION** Ngamiland District of northern Botswana, to the northern Kalahari Desert

**TYPE** Delta and swamp

**RIVER** Okavango

Covering about 400 sq miles (1,000 sq km), Vercors is the largest karst area in Europe. It has many long, deep caves, which contain a variety of tunnels, narrow streams, lakes, and waterfalls.

**LOCATION** Lower Alps of the Provence Alpes region, southeast France

**TYPE** Karst

**RIVERS** Drôme and Isère

# Lakes

Lakes are bodies of water that are created when surface water collects in a depression. Some are as shallow as a pond, while others are about half a mile (1 km) deep. Lakes may contain salt water or fresh water. Some have outlets to carry water away, while others do not.

## Great Slave Lake

The Great Slave Lake has a rocky shore with wide bays and many islands. Most of the land is covered with dense coniferous forests. This lake remains frozen for eight months of the year.

**LOCATION** Northwest Canada, east of the Mackenzie Mountains

**AREA** 11,029 sq miles (28,565 sq km)

**MAXIMUM DEPTH** 2,015 ft (615 m )

**OUTLET** Mackenzie River

## Great Bear Lake

The largest lake solely within Canadian territory, Great Bear Lake extends into the Arctic Circle in the north. The evergreen forests along its southern shores are home to grizzly bears.

**LOCATION** Northwest Canada, on the Arctic Circle

**AREA** 12,025 sq miles (31,150 sq km)

**MAXIMUM DEPTH** 1,465 ft (445 m)

**OUTLET** Great Bear River

# Great Salt Lake

This is the largest inland saltwater body in the western hemisphere. This lake has no outlet, so it can lose water only by evaporation, which leads to the buildup of minerals, making the lake extremely salty. It is surrounded by great areas of sand, salt flats, and salt marshes.

*Boulders coated with salt crystals*

**LOCATION**  Western Rocky Mountains, northern Utah

**AREA**  2,000 sq miles (5,000 sq km)

**MAXIMUM DEPTH**  39 ft (12 m)

**OUTLET**  None

# Lake Ladoga

Europe's largest lake, Ladoga lies in a hollow area gouged out by glaciers. The water is deepest near the high, rocky cliffs of the northern shores, while in the south, the lake is much shallower and has a low shoreline. The entire lake freezes between the months of January and May.

**LOCATION**  Karelia region of northwestern Russia, to the east of the Baltic Sea

**AREA**  6,825 sq miles (17,675 sq km)

**MAXIMUM DEPTH**  755 ft (230 m)

**OUTLET**  Neva River

## Lake Baikal

The oldest lake in the world, Baikal formed about 25 million years ago. It continues to widen at a rate of about 1 in (2½ cm) every year. It is also the Earth's deepest lake, containing 20 percent of the planet's entire surface fresh water.

**LOCATION** Russia, south of the Central Siberian Plateau, near Mongolia

**AREA** 12,160 sq miles (31,500 sq km)

**MAXIMUM DEPTH** 5,715 ft (1,740 m)

**OUTLET** Angara River

## Caspian Sea

The Caspian Sea is the Earth's largest inland body of water. It was once open sea, but got landlocked following the movement of tectonic plates. Its water level is constantly rising and falling due to climate change, which affects the level of the rivers flowing into it and the rate of evaporation.

## Dead Sea

**LOCATION** On the borders of Azerbaijan, Iran, Kazakhstan, Russia, and Turkmenistan

**AREA** 143,000 sq miles (371,000 sq km)

**MAXIMUM DEPTH** 3,120 ft (950 m)

**OUTLET** None

This is the world's lowest lake and, at 1,320 ft (400 m) below sea level, the lowest point on the Earth's surface. Because of the extremely high rate of evaporation, the Dead Sea is shrinking rapidly, its level lowering by about 3½ ft (1 m) every year. This evaporation also gives the lake a very high salt content—it is too salty, in fact, for anything to live in it, which is how it got its name.

**LOCATION** North of the Red Sea, bordered by Israel and Jordan

**AREA** 310 sq miles (810 sq km)

**MAXIMUM DEPTH** 1,085 ft (330 m)

**OUTLET** None

## Lake Vostok

This is the largest of all lakes discovered under Antarctica. It lies beneath blankets of ice up to 2½ miles (4 km) thick.

**LOCATION** Under the eastern Antarctic Ice Sheet

**AREA** 5,791 sq miles (15,000 sq km)

**MAXIMUM DEPTH** 3,000 ft (900 m)

**OUTLET** None

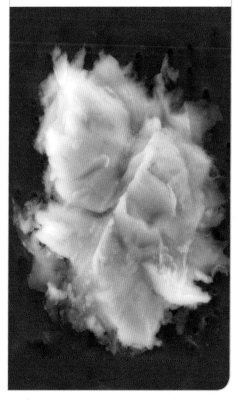

# Wetlands

When water collects on land and cannot drain, it builds up and forms flooded areas called wetlands. Lagoons are areas of shallow sea separated by islands or reefs, while swamps are wooded areas submerged in water. Marshes are similar to swamps, but they are covered with grasses and reeds.

## Great Dismal Swamp

The bottom of this swamp is covered with fallen trees and other plants. At its center is a circular freshwater lake called Lake Drummond. These wetlands are unusual in being located above sea level, whereas most swamps are found in low-lying natural basins or craters.

**LOCATION** About 25 miles (40 km) inland from the Atlantic Ocean, in North Carolina and Virginia

**TYPE** Swamp

**AREA** 600 sq miles (1,550 sq km)

## Everglades

Water flowing from Lake Okeechobee seeps slowly through the low-lying land toward the Gulf of Mexico. This creates a wetland with wide areas of sawgrass. The edges of this grass are so sharp they can cut through cloth.

**LOCATION** From Lake Okeechobee to Florida Bay, Florida

**TYPE** Swamp and marsh

**AREA** 4,000 sq miles (10,000 sq km)

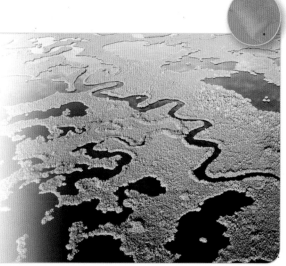

## Llanos wetlands

Every May, heavy rains flood the Llanos wetlands, creating islands of forests. These waterlogged areas are important habitats for water birds, supporting about 90 percent of the world's population of the endangered scarlet ibis.

**LOCATION** Orinoco River and its tributaries in western Venezuela

**TYPE** Swamp and marsh

**AREA** 4,000 sq miles (10,000 sq km)

## Pantanal

The world's largest freshwater wetland, the Pantanal occupies about a third of the upper basin of the Paraguay River. When the river floods every year, this swamp acts as a sponge and soaks up the excess water.

**LOCATION**  Mato Grosso and Mato Grosso do Sul states of Brazil, extending into Bolivia and Paraguay

**TYPE**  Swamp and marsh

**AREA**  50,000 sq miles (130,000 sq km)

## Camargue

This wetland is famous for its unique breed of white horses and for its birds, including greater flamingos and black-winged stilts.

**LOCATION**  Rhône Delta, France

**TYPE**  Lagoon and marsh

**AREA**  330 sq miles (850 sq km)

## Sudd

These marshes are a landscape of reed-beds and papyrus, with areas of water that are choked by dense mats of floating water hyacinth. An incomplete and abandoned canal project on its eastern side has left a huge trough, which blocks the migration of large mammals.

**LOCATION**  White Nile River, southern Sudan

**TYPE**  Marsh

**AREA**  13,300 sq miles (34,500 sq km)

## Sundarbans

This network of estuaries (wetlands where a river meets a sea) and tidal rivers surrounds flat, marshy islands covered with thick forests. The region supports a variety of wildlife, including spotted deer and the Bengal tiger.

**LOCATION** Between Kolkata, India, and Chittagong, Bangladesh

**TYPE** Swamp and marsh

**AREA** 685 sq miles (1,770 sq km)

## Coorong

The Coorong is a long, shallow lagoon that is separated from the Southern Ocean by a narrow sand dune peninsula. It is one of the best sites for bird-watching in Australia, as it is home to more than 230 species of bird.

**LOCATION** Mouth of the Murray River, Australia

**TYPE** Lagoon

**AREA** 80 sq miles (200 sq km)

# Glaciers

Glaciers are giant masses of ice formed by the piling up of snow over time. Most glaciers, except for massive icecaps and ice sheets, move down a mountain area and flow into a valley. When a glacier reaches the sea, chunks break off, forming icebergs.

## Hubbard Glacier

The Hubbard Glacier has been advancing for over a century. It threatens to block off a narrow strip of water near the Alaskan coast called Russell Fjord. If this fjord gets permanently blocked, it could overflow and flood the surrounding land.

## Malaspina Glacier

The Malaspina Glacier features the largest piedmont lobe in the world. This glacial type occurs when a valley glacier—formed when a glacier moves down a mountain into a valley—spreads out onto a low, flat area.

| | |
|---|---|
| **LOCATION** | Coast of St. Elias Mountains, Alaska |
| **TYPE** | Piedmont lobe |
| **AREA** | 1,500 sq miles (3,900 sq km) |

## Greenland Ice Sheet

Covering 80 percent of Greenland, this ice sheet is the largest ice mass in the northern hemisphere. Most northern Atlantic icebergs originate from this glacier, which contains 10 percent of the world's fresh water. It has an average thickness of 5,900 ft (1,790 m).

**LOCATION** St. Elias Mountains,
Canada, through southeastern Alaska

**TYPE** Valley glacier

**AREA** 1,350 sq miles (3,500 sq km)

## Vatnajökull Icecap

The largest glacier in Europe,
Vatnajökull completely covers the
mountainous Icelandic terrain it sits on.
It lies on top of several volcanoes. The heat
from these causes the icecap's base to melt,
creating lakes beneath it.

**LOCATION** Southeast Iceland

**TYPE** Icecap

**AREA** 3,100 sq miles (8,100 sq km)

**LOCATION** Greenland in the
Arctic Circle

**TYPE** Ice sheet

**AREA** 668,000 sq miles (1.73 million sq km)

## Antarctic Ice Sheet

The largest mass of ice on the Earth,
the Antarctic Ice Sheet weighs so much that
it pushes the Earth's crust down by about
2,955 ft (900 m). This glacier holds more
than 70 percent of the world's fresh water.

**LOCATION** Antarctica

**TYPE** Ice sheet

**AREA** 5.3 million sq miles (13.7 million sq km)

# Antarctic winters are

# so harsh

## that only a few birds, including emperor penguins, can breed during this time

**THE COOL COLONY**
To survive on the cold Antarctic Ice Sheet, emperor penguins form breeding colonies in areas that are sheltered from the wind by ice cliffs and icebergs. They also huddle together in groups, taking turns to move to the center so that each penguin stays warm.

# Glacial features

As glaciers move through and wear away mountainous regions, they create unique landforms. Great masses of ice can carve out valleys, flatten mountains, and pick up rocks and carry them for great distances. Some glacial features only become apparent when glaciers melt and disappear.

## Yorkshire boulder

Glaciers can carry huge boulders over large distances. The Yorkshire boulder was carried by a glacier and then dropped on top of younger rock when the glacier melted. Such rocks are known as erratics.

| | |
|---|---|
| **LOCATION** | Yorkshire, UK |
| **TYPE** | Erratic |
| **GLACIER** | Ice sheet |

## Muldalen hanging valley

Large glaciers are often fed by smaller flows of ice called tributary glaciers. While the large glacier gouges out a deep valley, the tributary carves a much smaller, higher "hanging valley" above the main valley. As with many hanging valleys, a waterfall sometimes flows from Muldalen down into the main valley.

| | |
|---|---|
| **LOCATION** | Muldalen, near Tafiord, Norway |
| **TYPE** | Hanging valley |
| **GLACIER** | Hanging valley glacier |

## Clew Bay

Drumlins are long, oval mounds of sediment that have been smoothed in the direction of a glacier's flow. In Clew Bay, clusters of drumlins appear as islands in the sea.

**LOCATION**  County Mayo, Ireland

**TYPE**  Drumlin

**GLACIER**  Valley glacier

## Gryllefjord cirque

A cirque is a curved, bowl-shaped feature at the head of a developing valley glacier. It is formed by erosion. The cirque at Gryllefjord has an arête— a long, thin ridge separating two cirques.

**LOCATION**  Gryllefjord, Norway

**TYPE**  Cirque

**GLACIER**  Cirque glacier

## Dolma La Pass lake

This lake in Dolma La Pass was formed when an ice block broke off from a glacier and got buried in the ground. It then melted, and created a kettle hole that filled with water to form a kettle lake.

**LOCATION**  Dolma La Pass, Tibet

**TYPE**  Kettle lake

**GLACIER**  Valley glacier

# Deserts

Areas of land that receive an average rainfall of less than 10 in (250 mm) a year are called deserts. Hot deserts have high temperatures year-round, while in cold deserts, the winters are freezing.

FOCUS ON...
## LAND FORMS
Deserts feature a variety of landscapes, from mountains and plateaus to plains.

## Great Basin Desert

Its high altitude and northerly position make the Great Basin Desert the only cold desert in the US. Its vegetation includes sagebrush, blackbrush, and shadscale, along with a few cacti.

**LOCATION**  Oregon, Idaho, Nevada, Utah, Wyoming, Colorado, and California

**TYPE**  Sandy and gravelly

**AREA**  158,000 sq miles (409,000 sq km)

**RAINFALL**  10 in (250 mm)

## Atacama Desert

This is the driest place on the Earth, and includes stretches of land where rain has never been recorded. In certain areas of this desert, coastal fogs form, providing some moisture for the growth of plants such as cacti.

**LOCATION**  The coast of northern Chile, west of the Andes, between Arica and Vallenar

**TYPE**  Rocky and salty

**AREA**  40,600 sq miles (105,200 sq km)

**RAINFALL**  Less than $3/5$ in (15 mm)

▲ In some deserts, wind covers the rocks in a dark coating called desert varnish. Many of these rocks feature ancient rock art.

▲ Inselbergs, also known as monadnocks, are isolated hills that stand out above the flat desert surface around them.

▲ Desert sand dunes are hills of sand made by wind blowing over the desert. They occur in varying shapes and sizes.

## Sahara Desert

The Sahara is the Earth's largest hot desert, covering an area about the size of the US. It has reddish sand and is famous for its ergs, or sand seas. These areas of sand can be up to 328 ft (100 m) deep, and feature different shapes of dunes.

**LOCATION** From the Atlantic Ocean to the Red Sea, covering most of northern Africa

**TYPE** Sandy, gravelly, and stony

**AREA** 3.5 million sq miles (9 million sq km)

**RAINFALL** ⁴/₅–16 in (20–400 mm)

## Namib Desert

The Namib Desert is situated on the coast, where moisture from sea fogs supports the growth of some unique plants. These include the *Welwitschia mirabilis*, which is famous for producing only two leaves in its lifetime that can span hundreds of years.

**LOCATION** Atlantic coast of Namibia, extending into southern Angola in the north

**TYPE** Gravelly and sandy

**AREA** 12,000 sq miles (31,000 sq km)

**RAINFALL** ³/₅–4 in (15–100 mm)

## Kalahari Desert

Sandwiched between the Orange River in the south and the Zambezi in the north, this desert is dominated by sandy ridges, along with dry lake beds and wide areas of salt-covered ground. The Kalahari is home to the nomadic San people, whose population is about 40,000.

**LOCATION**  Southern Botswana, extending west into Namibia and south into South Africa

**TYPE**  Sandy

**AREA**  350,000 sq miles (900,000 sq km)

**RAINFALL**  5–20 in (125–500 mm)

## Arabian Peninsula

The Arabian Peninsula contains some of the largest sandy desert areas in the world. This includes the Ar Rub 'al Khali, or Empty Quarter, in the south, which covers an area about the size of France.

**LOCATION**  From Syria to Yemen and Oman, east of the Red Sea

**TYPE**  Sandy and gravelly

**AREA**  900,000 sq miles (2.3 million sq km)

**RAINFALL**  2–8 in (50–200 mm)

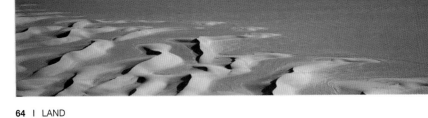

# Gobi Desert

Featuring a varied landscape, from rocky mountains to wide valleys and plains, the Gobi actually has very little sand. The central region of the desert is stony, with very little plant life, and the western region is extremely dry.

**LOCATION** Across southern Mongolia and the north of China as far as the Great Wall

**TYPE** Stony, gravelly, and sandy

**AREA** 500,000 sq miles (1.3 million sq km)

**RAINFALL** $^1/_2$–10 in (10–250 mm)

# Great Sandy Desert

As in most Australian deserts, the sand here is bright red because it is coated in iron oxides, which is similar to rust. The Great Sandy Desert is known for its dunes, which the wind constantly changes into new shapes.

**LOCATION** North of western Australia, extending as far as the Indian Ocean

**TYPE** Gravelly and sandy

**AREA** 130,000 sq miles (340,000 sq km)

**RAINFALL** 10–12 in (250–300 mm)

**LANDFORMS OF MOJAVE**
Found within the Mojave Desert of California,
Death Valley is the lowest, hottest, and driest
part of the North American continent. Large rocks,
called "sailing stones," appear to move across
the ground of this desert—no one knows how.

In Death Valley, giant 660 lb (300 kg) **stones move** mysteriously across the land, leaving trails on the ground

# Forests

A forest is an area with a high density of trees. Covering about 30 percent of the Earth's land surface, forests are found in regions with enough heat and rainfall to support tree growth. The trees provide oxygen and food-rich habitats for a wide variety of animals.

Forests are made up of two main types of tree—evergreen and deciduous.

▲ Evergreen trees, such as pine trees, never shed all their leaves. They remain green throughout the year.

▲ Maple, birch, and other deciduous trees shed their leaves in the fall and remain bare all winter. The leaves grow back in the spring.

**North American boreal forest**

Boreal forests are found in the colder parts of the northern hemisphere. The North American boreal forest is covered in snow for most of the year. Its tree canopy consists mainly of black and white spruce, as these trees can survive this extreme cold. It is bordered to the north by the Arctic tundra, where conditions are too harsh to support tree growth.

| | |
|---|---|
| **LOCATION** | Central Alaska to central Labrador, Canada |
| **TYPE** | Boreal forest |
| **AREA** | 2.4 million sq miles (6.25 million sq km) |

## California coniferous forest

These forests are famous for being home to the world's largest tree species—the giant sequoia. These trees may grow for over 2,000 years and reach almost 328 ft (100 m) in height.

**LOCATION** Sierra Nevada, California

**TYPE** Evergreen temperate forest

**AREA** 16,800 sq miles (43,600 sq km)

## Pacific northwest forest

High rainfall and coastal fogs create ideal conditions for the growth of some huge trees in this forest, such as the redwood, Douglas fir, sitka spruce, and western hemlock.

**LOCATION** The Gulf of Alaska to northern California and Canada

**TYPE** Temperate rainforest

**AREA** 463,000 sq miles (1.2 million sq km)

## Amazon rainforest

The largest area of tropical rainforest in the world, the Amazon rainforest covers much of the basin of the Amazon River. More than half of the world's species of plant, animal, and insect live in this rainforest.

**LOCATION** From the Andes, South America, to the Atlantic Ocean

**TYPE** Tropical rainforest

**AREA** 2.3 million sq miles (6 million sq km)

Some tribes living deep inside the Amazon rainforest have never had contact with the outside world.

## European mixed forest

This type of forest occurs in much of the lowland and hill country in Europe, particularly in Central Europe. Depending on the weather pattern, type of soil, and drainage of rainwater, a variety of trees grow here, including oak, beech, lime, ash, elm, birch, and alder.

**LOCATION** From the British Isles to western Russia

**TYPE** Deciduous temperate and evergreen temperate forests

**AREA** 1.6 million sq miles (4 million sq km)

## Eurasian boreal forest

## Central African rainforest

The rainforests of central Africa make up more than 80 percent of the continent's total area of rainforest. About 11,000 plant species, and more than 400 species of mammal, are found in the rainforests of the Democratic Republic of Congo. The mountain forests of Uganda, Rwanda, and Burundi are home to the famous mountain gorilla.

**LOCATION** Cameroon, Equatorial Guinea; and Gabon to Uganda and Burundi

**TYPE** Tropical rainforest

**AREA** 733,000 sq miles (1.9 million sq km)

Although this forest consists mostly of evergreen conifers, such as the Norway spruce and the Scots pine, some parts of the forest support deciduous trees such as larch, birch, alder, and rowan. Some areas even feature a mix of both types of tree growing together.

**LOCATION** Western Scandinavia, across northern Europe and Asia, to the Pacific Ocean

**TYPE** Boreal forest

**AREA** 3.4 million sq miles (8.75 million sq km)

# Madagascan rainforest

Most of this rainforest lies on the eastern side of the island of Madagascar, which broke off from mainland Africa about 135 million years ago. Because of the island's isolation, about 80 percent of its plants and 95 percent of its 300 reptile species—including two-thirds of the world's chameleons—are not found anywhere else.

**LOCATION** Masoala Peninsula, Madagascar

**TYPE** Tropical rainforest

**AREA** 14,670 sq miles (38,000 sq km)

## Northeast Asian mixed forest

This mixed forest mostly features cedar pine, black fir, and local species of spruce, ash, maple, linden, and walnut. Its wildlife includes mammals such as the musk deer and the rare Siberian tiger.

**LOCATION**   Northeast China, through Korea, southeast Russia, and northern Japan

**TYPE**   Deciduous temperate and evergreen temperate forests

**AREA**   1.2 million sq miles (3.2 million sq km)

## Northeast Australian rainforest

This forest grows on the eastern slopes of the country's coastal mountain ranges, where the average annual rainfall is more than 59 in (150 cm). Its trees range from 65 ft (20 m) to 130 ft (40 m) tall.

**LOCATION** Northeast Queensland, from Cape York south to the Connors Range

**TYPE** Tropical rainforest

**AREA** 4,000 sq miles (10,500 sq km)

## Wollemi pine forest

The Wollemi pine is a survivor from a 200 million-year-old group of plants. It was thought to be extinct—with the youngest fossils dating back two million years—until 1994, when a living plant was discovered in an isolated part of Australia. Fewer than 100 adult trees are known to exist in the wild.

**LOCATION** Western edge of the Sydney Basin, Australia

**TYPE** Temperate rainforest

**AREA** I imited and secret location within the Wollemi National Park

# Grasslands

Grasslands are areas where there is not enough rain for many trees to grow, but there is enough to prevent deserts from forming. There are two types—temperate grasslands, which have hot summers, cold winters, and year-round rainfall; and tropical grasslands, or savanna, which have wet and dry seasons.

## Great Plains

The Great Plains is by far the largest area of grassland in North America. Its land is so fertile that most of it is now used for agriculture. Only one percent is still in its natural, wild state.

**LOCATION**  North America, between the Rocky Mountains and Mississippi River

**TYPE**  Temperate

**AREA**  1.2 million sq miles (3 million sq km)

## Pampas

This huge plain has varying landscapes. The eastern side has a mild climate all year round, and features pampas grass, which is known for its tall stems with silky, featherlike flowers. Toward the Andes, the land is extremely dry and turns into a semi-desert.

**LOCATION**  Northern Argentina and Uruguay, from the Andes foothills to the Atlantic Ocean

**TYPE**  Temperate

**AREA**  270,000 sq miles (700,000 sq km)

## Serengeti Plains

These plains feature a mix of grasslands and forests, and have the largest populations of grazing animals in Africa. Every summer, when the grasses dry up, more than 1.3 million blue wildebeest, 200,000 zebras, and 40,000 Thomson's gazelles migrate across the Serengeti in search of fresh grass and drinking water.

**LOCATION**  From northwest Tanzania, east of Lake Victoria, to southwest Kenya

**TYPE**  Tropical

**AREA**  8,900 sq miles (23,000 sq km)

## Central Asian steppes

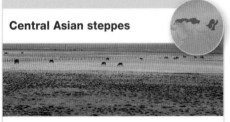

Extreme changes in temperature are common in this region, but animals here are adapted to cope. For example, saiga antelope develop a thick, woolly coat to keep warm in the winter and a thin, reddish coat during the summer.

**LOCATION**  From Ukraine, through Russia and Kazakhstan to Mongolia and China

**TYPE**  Temperate

**AREA**  965,000 sq miles (2.5 million sq km)

## Australian savanna

Made up of dense, scattered trees, the savanna forms a band between the hot desert interior of Australia and the forests on its north coast. The region has cool, dry winters, and hot, humid summers.

**LOCATION**  North of western Australia, through Northern Territory, into Queensland

**TYPE**  Tropical

**AREA**  463,500 sq miles (1.2 million sq km)

# Tundra

The term tundra is used to describe a vast and almost treeless landscape that covers about 20 percent of the Earth's land surface. The ground remains frozen for most of the year. In some areas, the top layer thaws during the spring and the summer. Where the ground remains frozen for at least two years, it is known as permafrost.

## North American tundra

Although it is mostly flat and barren, the North American tundra does feature some landforms such as polygons (geometrical patterns on the soil), pingos (ice mounds), and even a few mountain ranges. In the spring, the ice and snow melt to show lichens, mosses, and Arctic flowers.

**LOCATION** From Alaska through northern Canada; Greenland's coastal regions

**AREA** 2 million sq miles (5.3 million sq km)

**TEMPERATURE** -76°F–75°F (-60°C–24°C)

**RAINFALL** 2–8 in (50–200 mm)

## Eurasian tundra

This region features a variety of landscapes, from the freezing damp plains of Siberia to the island groups of the southern Arctic Ocean. A number of small, long-lived plants, such as mosses and rushes, are found here. These plants grow only during a short, 90-day period from May to July. Many migratory animals arrive during these warmer months.

**LOCATION** From Iceland in the west, through northern Scandinavia, Russia, and Siberia

**AREA** 1.3 million sq miles (3.3 million sq km)

**TEMPERATURE** -76°F–77°F (-60°C–25°C)

**RAINFALL** 8–12 in (200–300 mm)

During the summer, more than 200 million breeding birds, including ducks and geese, migrate to the Eurasian tundra.

## TUNDRA COLORS

In the tundra, the temperature rises during the summer, and the frozen topsoil melts to form small pools. The ground thaws just enough to allow plants to reproduce, before the winter sets in. When the spring arrives, these plants flower, and the region shows splashes of color.

In the summer, **the Sun never sets** over the tundra

# Agricultural areas

Farming began in the Middle East around 10,000 years ago, and today, it actively involves two billion people worldwide. Farming can be arable (growing crops) or pastoral (rearing livestock such as cattle and pigs). Farming practices depend on many things, including climate, altitude, soil condition, economics, and local traditions.

## Cereal cultivation

The first plants to be domesticated were cereals—grasses that are grown for their edible seeds or grains. Cereals are an important source of energy and are grown in large quantities. Wheat, rice, and corn together account for over half the world's food. Other popular cereals are rye, oats, and barley.

| | |
|---|---|
| **TYPE** | Arable |
| **AREA** | 14 million sq miles (36 million sq km) |
| **MAIN COUNTRIES** | China, US, India, and Russia |

## Cattle farming

Cattle are an important source of meat, but are also kept for their milk. The largest cattle farms are found where there are vast areas of open land, such as North America, South America, and Australia.

| | |
|---|---|
| **TYPE** | Pastoral |
| **AREA** | 11.2 million sq miles (29 million sq km) |
| **MAIN COUNTRIES** | US, China, Brazil, Argentina, and Australia |

## Rice cultivation

Growing rice requires lots of water. In hilly areas, rice is grown in terraces—levels cut into the hillsides to keep soil and water in place. Rice was first cultivated in Asia, which remains the world's largest producer of this crop.

**TYPE** Arable

**AREA** 4.6 million sq miles (12 million sq km)

**MAIN COUNTRIES** China, India, Indonesia, Bangladesh, and Vietnam

## Plantation agriculture

A plantation is a large estate where only one type of crop is grown. Most large-scale commercial crops that are grown in warm climates are produced in plantations. These include tea, coffee, bananas, palm oil, cocoa, sugar cane, and cotton.

**TYPE** Arable

**AREA** 3.1 million sq miles (8 million sq km)

**MAIN COUNTRIES** Malaysia, Brazil, Mexico, India, and Cuba

## Mixed farming

In this type of farming, farmers grow and rear a range of crops and livestock, rather than concentrating on a single product. This reduces farmer's risk of losses, for example, if a particular crop gets infected or if animals get sick.

**TYPE** Arable and pastoral

**AREA** 21 million sq miles (54 million sq km)

**MAIN COUNTRIES** China, India, US, Russia, and France

# Urban areas

Today, half the world's population live in urban areas—cities and towns—rather than in the countryside. About three percent of the Earth's land surface is urban, and this figure is likely to double over the next 20 years. Cities are centers of culture, transportation, trade, and technology.

## São Paulo

One of the world's fastest-growing cities, São Paulo is located near large deposits of iron ore, which led to its industrial development. Its links to Santos, the busiest port in Latin America, make it a major center of transportation.

| | |
|---|---|
| **COUNTRY** | Brazil |
| **AREA** | 585 sq miles (1,525 sq km) |
| **POPULATION** | 11.3 million |

## New York City

The largest city in the US, New York is one of the world's leading cultural and financial centers. It is also famous for its skyline, which is made up of many extremely tall buildings called skyscrapers, such as the Empire State Building.

| | |
|---|---|
| **COUNTRY** | US |
| **AREA** | 470 sq miles (1,215 sq km) |
| **POPULATION** | 8.2 million |

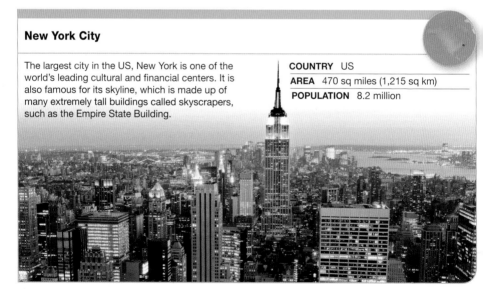

## London

The city of London was established by the Romans more than 2,000 years ago. It is located on the Thames River, which is famous for the many bridges built over it, including Tower Bridge. The capital city of the UK, London is a global center of finance and theater.

**COUNTRY** UK

**AREA** 605 sq miles (1,570 sq km)

**POPULATION** 12.8 million

## New Delhi

As India's capital city, New Delhi is a key political, financial, and industrial center. The Rashtrapati Bhavan—the official residence of the president of India—is located here, as are other important government buildings.

**COUNTRY** India

**AREA** 575 sq miles (1,485 sq km)

**POPULATION** 12.3 million

## Tokyo

The city of Tokyo is part of a huge urban area with more than 30 million inhabitants. It is often affected by earthquakes because it is located where four tectonic plates meet.

**COUNTRY** Japan

**AREA** 845 sq miles (2,190 sq km)

**POPULATION** 13.2 million

# Ocean

Oceans cover about two-thirds of the Earth's surface, at an average depth of 12,100 ft (3,700 m). The Earth's oceans formed more than three billion years ago. Until the first life-forms emerged onto land 450 million years ago, life was found only in the oceans. Over time, the oceans have grown and shrunk as the Earth's internal forces have moved the continents around. The movement of heat and moisture between the oceans and the atmosphere plays a crucial role in shaping the world's climates.

**A GLOW IN THE DARK**
Many sea animals, such as this comb jelly, produce light in the dark depths of the ocean. This light helps them to find and attract prey, or to signal to other animals.

# Ocean currents

Ocean water is constantly moving, both at the surface and far below the waves, circulating warm water from the equator and cold water from the poles. The patterns of this movement are called ocean currents. These currents are influenced by several factors, including the Earth's rotation, the winds, and tidal changes in sea level.

## Currents and gyres

The combination of wind blowing over the oceans and the rotation of the Earth makes surface water swirl clockwise in the northern hemisphere and counterclockwise in the southern hemisphere. These swirling patterns, called gyres, carry warm tropical water away from the equator and colder water toward it.

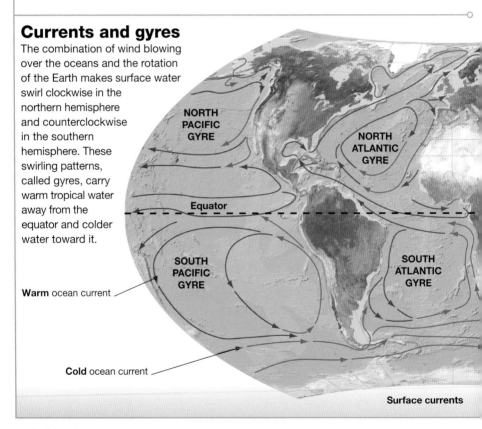

NORTH PACIFIC GYRE

NORTH ATLANTIC GYRE

Equator

SOUTH PACIFIC GYRE

SOUTH ATLANTIC GYRE

**Warm** ocean current

**Cold** ocean current

**Surface currents**

## Global Conveyor Belt

Cold deep-water currents and warm surface currents all link together, distributing heat around the globe. This system is often called the Global Conveyor Belt.

Warm **surface current**

Cold, salty **deep-water current**

**SOUTH INDIAN GYRE**

## Meeting of currents

The movement of water at the ocean's surface is called a surface current. When cold water flows deep down, it stirs up seabed nutrients, which comes up to the ocean's surface. This provides good feeding grounds for sea animals.

# Seas and oceans

The Earth has five oceans. Around their edges are smaller bodies of water, including seas, bays, and gulfs. Together, oceans and seas cover more than two-thirds of the Earth's surface. Below the waves, the ocean floors are made up of various features, such as mountain ranges, deep plains and trenches, and coral reefs.

## Arctic Ocean

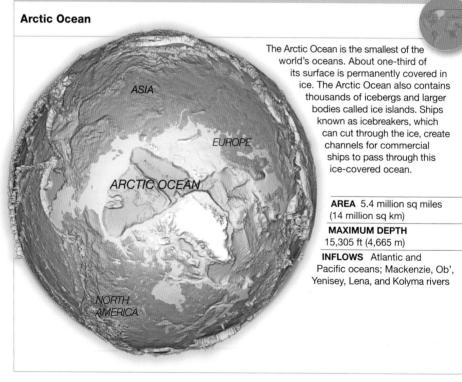

The Arctic Ocean is the smallest of the world's oceans. About one-third of its surface is permanently covered in ice. The Arctic Ocean also contains thousands of icebergs and larger bodies called ice islands. Ships known as icebreakers, which can cut through the ice, create channels for commercial ships to pass through this ice-covered ocean.

**AREA** 5.4 million sq miles (14 million sq km)

**MAXIMUM DEPTH** 15,305 ft (4,665 m)

**INFLOWS** Atlantic and Pacific oceans; Mackenzie, Ob', Yenisey, Lena, and Kolyma rivers

## Chukchi Sea

Water low in salt content flows from the Pacific Ocean into the colder, more saline (salty) water of the Chukchi Sea. Rich in nutrients, this mixed water supports a wide variety of marine life, which includes large populations of walrus and several species of seals.

**AREA** 225,000 sq miles (582,000 sq km)

**MAXIMUM DEPTH** 360 ft (110 m)

**INFLOWS** Bering and East Siberian seas, and Arctic Basin

## Barents Sea

Unlike other Arctic seas, the Barents Sea remains mostly ice-free through the year. Its floor is rich in invertebrates, such as sea cucumbers, feather stars, and starfish.

**AREA** 542,000 sq miles (1.4 million sq km)

**MAXIMUM DEPTH** 2,000 ft (600 m)

**INFLOWS** Norwegian Sea and Arctic Basin

## White Sea

The White Sea is an almost landlocked part of the Arctic Ocean. Its floor is broken up by troughs and ridges.

**AREA** 35,000 sq miles (90,000 sq km)

**MAXIMUM DEPTH** 1,115 ft (340 m)

**INFLOWS** Barents Sea; Onega and Northern Dvina rivers

## Atlantic Ocean

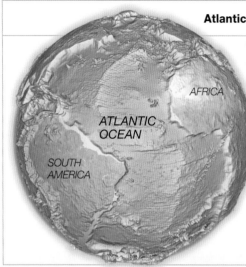

The world's second largest ocean, the Atlantic has several tributary seas. A massive mountain range, called the Mid-Atlantic Ridge, covers almost one-third of the ocean floor. The range has basins on either side, some of which contain large volcanoes.

**AREA** 29.7 million sq miles (77 million sq km)

**MAXIMUM DEPTH** 28,230 ft (8,605 m)

**INFLOWS** Arctic and Southern oceans; Mediterranean Sea; St. Lawrence, Mississippi, Orinoco, Amazon, Paraná, Congo, Niger, Loire, and Rhine rivers

## Black Sea

An almost landlocked body of water, the Black Sea mostly occupies a deep, broad basin separating Europe from Asia.

**AREA** 163,000 sq miles (422,000 sq km)

**MAXIMUM DEPTH** 7,200 ft (2,200 m)

**INFLOWS** Sea of Azov, Mediterranean Sea; Danube, Dniester, Dnieper, and Kizil Irmak rivers

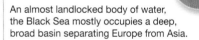

## Mediterranean Sea

The world's largest inland sea, the Mediterranean was separated from the Atlantic Ocean to the west when the Earth's sea level dropped, about six million years ago. Over the next two million years, the region flooded, the water levels rose, and the sea linked to the Atlantic again.

## Baltic Sea

About 8,000 years ago, the ice sheet that covered Scandinavia melted, submerging the region under water. The Baltic Sea is what remains of that water. Nine countries have their coastline on this sea.

**AREA**  149,000 sq miles (386,000 sq km)

**MAXIMUM DEPTH**  1,475 ft (450 m)

**INFLOWS**  Vistula, Oder, and Western Dvina rivers

**AREA**  965,000 sq miles (2.5 million sq km)

**MAXIMUM DEPTH**  16,075 ft (4,900 m)

**INFLOWS**  Atlantic Ocean; Black Sea; Nile, Rhône, Po, and Ebro rivers

## Hudson Bay

This large, shallow body of water has a rocky eastern coast with high cliffs, but its other shores are marshy and low. High amounts of nutrients are dissolved in its waters. These support a variety of creatures, including beluga whales, which enter the bay during the summer season.

**AREA**  316,000 sq miles (819,000 sq km)

**MAXIMUM DEPTH**  886 ft (270 m)

**INFLOWS**  Albany, Churchill, Moose, Nelson, Severn, and Grande Rivière de la Baleine rivers

## Sargasso Sea

This is the only sea of the northern Atlantic that is not bordered by land. It is created by three currents around its edge—the Canaries Current, the North Equatorial Current, and the Gulf Stream. The Sargasso Sea is named for the wide mats of sargassum, a yellow-brown seaweed, that float on its surface. This seaweed supports a variety of animal life.

| | |
|---|---|
| **AREA** | 2 million sq miles (5.2 million sq km) |
| **MAXIMUM DEPTH** | 23,000 ft (7,000 m) |
| **INFLOWS** | None |

*The sargassum seaweed has tiny gas-filled bladders, allowing it to float on the water surface*

## Gulf of Mexico

This oval basin contains mostly shallow waters. Mangrove swamps, tidal marshes, beaches, lagoons, and estuaries are found along its coasts. The Mississippi River carries a huge volume of sand and silt into the Gulf of Mexico. These sediments are deposited on the seafloor, forming an enormous fan-shaped delta with wide salt marshes.

| | |
|---|---|
| **AREA** | 615,000 sq miles (1.6 million sq km) |
| **MAXIMUM DEPTH** | 17,060 ft (5,200 m) |
| **INFLOWS** | Caribbean Sea; Mississippi, Brazos, Colorado, Alabama, Apalachicola, and Rio Grande rivers |

## Caribbean Sea

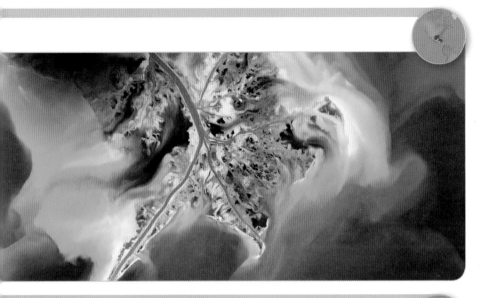

The sea, its numerous islands—many of which are volcanic—and neighboring coastlines make up the Caribbean region. Most of the islands, as well as some of the mainland coasts, are lined with coral reefs that support a rich variety of fish and invertebrates, including spiny lobsters and conches.

**AREA**  1.1 million sq miles (2.75 million sq km)

**MAXIMUM DEPTH**  25,215 ft (7,685 m )

**INFLOWS**  Atlantic Ocean; Magdalena, Coco, Patuca, and Motagua rivers

# Indian Ocean

Formed over the last 120 million years, the Indian Ocean is one of the world's youngest ocean basins. Its mostly warm waters create ideal conditions for a large variety of marine life. Twice every year, the monsoon winds reverse the flow of its currents, bringing up nutrient-rich water from the ocean's depths. This pattern is unique to the Indian Ocean.

**AREA** 26.5 million sq miles (69 million sq km)

**MAXIMUM DEPTH** 23,815 ft (7,260 m )

**INFLOWS** Ganges, Indus, Tigris, Euphrates, Zambezi, Limpopo, and Murray rivers

# Arabian Sea

The Arabian Sea occupies the northwestern part of the Indian Ocean. In addition to supporting a huge fishing industry, it is also an important trade route linking the Red Sea with the Persian Gulf.

**AREA** 1.5 million sq miles (3.9 million sq km)

**MAXIMUM DEPTH** 19,030 ft (5,800 m)

**INFLOWS** Indus and Narmada rivers

## Andaman Sea

Southeast of the Bay of Bengal, the Andaman Sea is separated from the bay by the Andaman and Nicobar islands. This region is close to three tectonic plates—the India plate, the Burma plate, and the Sunda Megathrust—and is often affected by earthquakes.

**AREA**  308,000 sq miles (798,000 sq km)

**MAXIMUM DEPTH**  12,390 ft (3,775 m)

**INFLOWS**  Bay of Bengal, Strait of Malacca; Irriwaddy and Salween rivers

## Persian Gulf

This warm, salty sea is known for the huge oil reserves found beneath its floor. Its eastern shore is mountainous, while its western shore has many islands, lagoons, and tidal flats. Many artificial islands have been built along its coast, such as the Palm Islands in the UAE, which are shaped like palm trees.

**AREA**  93,000 sq miles (241,000 sq km)

**MAXIMUM DEPTH**  360 ft (110 m)

**INFLOWS**  Tigris, Euphrates, and Karun rivers

## Pacific Ocean

The largest ocean in the world, the Pacific covers more than one-third of the Earth's surface and contains the deepest point in the Earth's oceans—Challenger Deep in the Mariana Trench. This ocean is located in a geologically active area—most of the planet's earthquakes occur in the Pacific Ring of Fire, a long, horseshoe-shaped active belt in the ocean's basin.

**AREA**  60 million sq miles (156 million sq km)

**MAXIMUM DEPTH**  35,840 ft (10,925 m)

**INFLOWS**  Southern Ocean; Yukon, Columbia, Amur, Yellow, Yangtze, and Mekong rivers

## Sea of Okhotsk

The Sea of Okhotsk was created over the last two million years by the erosion of land by glaciers. This large, cold sea freezes during the winter and is frequently covered with fog. It is almost completely surrounded by Russian territory.

**AREA**  615,000 sq miles (1.6 million sq km )

**MAXIMUM DEPTH**  11,060 ft (3,370 m)

**INFLOWS**  Sea of Japan; Amur, Uda, Okhota, and Penzhina rivers

## South China Sea

The South China Sea stretches for more than 1,680 miles (2,700 km) around Asia's mainland. The Gulf of Thailand, which branches out from the sea, has 42 forest-covered islands, which rise from the sea as rock formations. These islands make up a marine park called the Ang Thong National Park.

**AREA** 1.4 million sq miles (3.7 million sq km)

**MAXIMUM DEPTH** 16,455 ft (5,015 m)

**INFLOWS** Xi Jiang, Mekong, Red, Tha Chin, and Chao Phraya rivers

## Coral Sea

Famous for the world's largest coral reef—the Great Barrier Reef—the Coral Sea also contains many individual reefs and small islands, collectively called the Coral Sea Islands Territory. This sea has a tropical climate, with frequent typhoons (violent tropical storms) between January and April.

**AREA** 1.8 million sq miles (4.8 million sq km)

**MAXIMUM DEPTH** 30,070 ft (9,165 m)

**INFLOWS** West central Pacific Ocean; Fly, Purari, and Kikori rivers

## Southern Ocean

This ocean is also known as the Antarctic Ocean because it completely surrounds Antarctica. It has the strongest winds found anywhere on the Earth. These, along with many icebergs and large waves, make ship navigation in this sea very dangerous.

**AREA** 7.8 million sq miles (20 million sq km)

**MAXIMUM DEPTH** 23,735 ft (7,235 m)

**INFLOWS** Summer melting of sea-ice and icebergs calved from Antarctic ice shelves

*SOUTHERN OCEAN*

*ANTARCTICA*

*SOUTHERN OCEAN*

## Scotia Sea

This cold sea lies between the southern Atlantic Ocean and the Southern Ocean. Icebergs from the Antarctic Ice Sheet can be found here all year round, and in the winter, sea-ice forms at the region's edges.

**AREA** 350,000 sq miles (900,000 sq km)

**MAXIMUM DEPTH** 13,000 ft (4,000 m)

**INFLOWS** Southern Ocean to the west of Drake Passage

## Ross Sea

Of all the seas around Antarctica, the Ross Sea has the least sea-ice, making it very accessible to shipping. The sea is home to the icefish, which has a special protein in its body that prevents it from freezing.

**AREA**  370,000 sq miles (960,000 sq km)

**MAXIMUM DEPTH**  8,200 ft (2,500 m)

**INFLOWS**  Icebergs calved from the Ross Ice Shelf

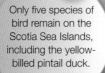

## Weddell Sea

Heavily covered in ice, this sea is home to the Weddell seal, which swims beneath the ice and can break through to the surface to create breathing holes. Colonies of emperor penguins are also found in this sea.

**AREA**  1.1 million sq miles (2.8 million sq km)

**MAXIMUM DEPTH**  10,000 ft (3,000 m)

**INFLOWS**  Icebergs calved from the Ronne-Filchner Ice shelf

Only five species of bird remain on the Scotia Sea Islands, including the yellow-billed pintail duck.

**DISAPPEARING ISLAND**
The Pacific Ocean is dotted with volcanoes that once erupted from the ocean floor but are now extinct. Bora Bora island is one of these volcanoes. As its deep source of heat cools and the rocks contract, the island is slowly sinking back beneath the waves.

The four-million-year-old
tropical island of Bora Bora

# is sinking

at the rate of ½ in (1 cm)

every 100 years

# What is a coral reef?

Coral reefs are wave-resistant structures made by marine creatures and their skeletons. These colorful formations are home to an incredible range of plants and animals, including sponges, worms, anemones, and mollusks such as snails, clams, and octopuses. The richest and healthiest reefs support thousands of fish and turtles.

## Formation of coral reefs

Although coral reefs can be huge—stretching for up to hundreds of miles—the organisms that form them are very small. Corals are made up of tiny individual creatures called polyps. As they grow, polyps create a hard outer shell, or skeleton, of limestone. When they die, this shell remains, and new polyps grow on it. In this way, reefs are formed and continue to grow.

# TYPES OF REEF

A **fringing reef** is formed as corals grow around an island or along a shoreline.

A **barrier reef** runs parallel to the shore but is separated from it by a large lagoon.

An **atoll** is a ring of coral reefs or low-lying coral islands that surrounds a shallow lagoon.

**Coral bleaching**

## Coral damage

Today, coral reefs face many threats to their survival. Pollution and rising water temperatures can kill corals, which lose color when they die—this is known as coral bleaching. Reefs are also damaged by human activity, such as using dynamite to catch fish.

## POLYPS

Corals are made up of tiny individual creatures known as polyps.

▲ Some polyps attach themselves to the seafloor or rocks using parts called basal plates.

▲ Polyps' tentacles have stinging cells, which are used to sting, paralyze, and catch prey.

▲ The tentacles surround and move food to the polyp's mouth. Its gut secretes the limestone that builds the reef.

# Coral reefs

Among the Earth's most spectacular and diverse habitats, coral reefs support more species per unit of area than any other marine environment. They also protect islands and coasts from erosion.

## Bahama Banks

A cluster of 700 islands make up the Bahama Banks. These islands are scattered over two limestone platforms— the Little Bahama Banks and the Great Bahama Banks. These platforms have been growing for the last 70 million years.

**LOCATION** Bahamas, southeast of Florida, and northeast of Cuba

**TYPE** Fringing reef, patch reef, and barrier reef

**AREA** 1,200 sq miles (3,150 sq km)

## Lighthouse Reef

The coral formations of the Lighthouse Reef surround a large, circular sinkhole known as the Great Blue Hole. The sinkhole is about 480 ft (145 m) deep and features a number of ancient stalactites hanging from its slanting walls.

**LOCATION**  Western Caribbean, 60 miles (80 km) east of central Belize

**TYPE**  Atoll with patch reef

**AREA**  116 sq miles (300 sq km)

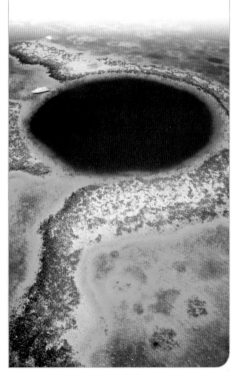

## Aldabra Atoll

The largest raised coral atoll in the world, Aldabra is situated on top of an ancient volcanic peak. Strong ocean tides in Aldabra's lagoon have turned raised clumps of reef into small, mushroom-shaped islands known as champignons.

**LOCATION**  Western end of the Republic of Seychelles archipelago, northwestern Madagascar

**TYPE**  Atoll

**AREA**  60 sq miles (155 sq km)

## Maldives

The Maldives are a group of islands with 26 atolls, many of which contain mini-atolls, called faros, which are rare outside the Maldives. Due to climate change over the past century, the Maldives may be under threat from rising sea levels—the highest island is less than 10 ft (3 m) above sea level.

**LOCATION**  Southwest of Sri Lanka, in the Indian Ocean

**TYPE**  Atoll and fringing reef

**AREA**  3,500 sq miles (9,000 sq km)

# Red Sea reefs

The Red Sea contains a variety of reefs. The northern area has mostly fringing reefs, with reef flats (flat areas of reef next to the shore) only a few yards wide, while the southern Red Sea has a much wider area of shallow continental shelf—the underwater extension of a continent. The Red Sea reefs are home to a spectacular range of corals and fish, including the Red Sea lionfish.

**LOCATION** Red Sea coasts of Egypt, Israel, Jordan, Saudi Arabia, Sudan, Eritrea, and Yemen

**TYPE** Fringing reef, patch reef, and barrier reef, and atoll

**AREA** 6,300 sq miles (16,500 sq km)

## Nusa Tenggara

This is a chain of about 500 coral-fringed islands. The islands in the north are volcanic in origin, while those in the south are mainly made up of coral limestone. Nusa Tenggara supports a huge variety of marine life—a single large reef can contain more species of fish than all the European seas combined.

**LOCATION**  Southern Indonesia, from Lombok in the west to Timor in the east

**TYPE**  Fringing reef and barrier reef

**AREA**  2,000 sq miles (5,000 sq km)

## Great Barrier Reef

The Great Barrier Reef is often described as the largest structure ever made by living organisms. It is made up of about 3,000 individual reefs and small coral islands. It has the world's largest collection of coral reefs, with 400 types of coral, 1,500 species of fish, and 4,000 types of mollusk.

**LOCATION**  Parallel to Queensland coast, northeastern Australia

**TYPE**  Barrier reef

**AREA**  14,300 sq miles (37,000 sq km)

# Even after a coral dies, its hard
# skeleton remains
## and new corals grow on it

**REEF BUILDING**

Many organisms, such as algae, corals, and mollusks, help form the foundation of a coral reef. The force of the waves and the grazing of animals help break the animal shells into sand, which fills the gaps in the growing reef. Algae bind it all together to form reef rock.

# Coastal features

A broad area of land that borders the sea is called a coast. Coasts can feature gulfs, lagoons, dunes, and beaches. These are formed by different processes such as the flow of tides, breaking waves, or the buildup of sediments.

▲ Land-based processes include the flow of glaciers, lava, and sediment, as well as human activity.

▲ Marine-based processes include waves, tides, currents, and changing sea levels.

### Oregon National Dunes

This is the largest area of coastal sand dunes in North America. The dunes were formed by a combination of erosion by sea waves, and the transport of sand by ocean winds over millions of years. Winds continue to mold the sand dunes into wavelike shapes.

| | |
|---|---|
| **LOCATION** | Southwest of Portland, Oregon |
| **TYPE** | Coastal dunes |
| **SIZE** | 40 miles (65 km) |

## Dungeness Spit

A spit is a narrow strip of land connected to the coast at one end. This spit is named after Dungeness in England. Its unique shape was formed by winds blowing from different directions in different seasons.

**LOCATION**  Seattle, Washington

**TYPE**  Sand spit

**SIZE**  5½ miles (9 km)

## Gulf of Bothnia

As the surrounding land rises, the sea level falls by about $\frac{1}{3}$ in (7 mm) a year in this northern arm of the Baltic Sea, revealing new islands along the coast. The water has a low salt content because of the large amount of fresh water that flows into it.

**LOCATION**  Between Finland's west coast and Sweden's east coast

**TYPE**  Gulf

**SIZE**  45,200 sq miles (117,000 sq km)

## White Cliffs of Dover

Coastal erosion by waves and tides has eaten into the soft white limestone that forms the chalk cliffs of Dover. The chalk is made of countless tiny skeletons of marine microorganisms along with some larger fossil shells.

**LOCATION**  Dover, UK

**TYPE**  Marine-based coast

**SIZE**  11 miles (17 km)

## Durdle Door

This limestone arch used to be a cliff. Sea waves wore away the softer layers of rock at the bottom of the cliff, leaving the harder rock at the top, creating an arch.

**LOCATION**   Dorset, southern UK
**TYPE**   Arch
**SIZE**   200 ft (60 m) high

## Skeleton Coast

This arid (dry) region has low gravel plains in the south, while in the north, sand dunes extend to the sea. Due to strong winds, the shapes of the dunes are constantly changing.

**LOCATION**   Northwest Windhoek, Namibia
**TYPE**   Marine-based coast
**SIZE**   310 miles (500 km)

## Kerala backwaters

These slow-moving stretches of water are made up of a chain of lagoons and small lakes linked by canals. Fed by 38 rivers, the backwaters cover almost half the length of the state of Kerala.

**LOCATION**   Southeast Cochin, Kerala, India
**TYPE**   Lagoon
**SIZE**   400 sq miles (1,000 sq km)

## Kinabatangan mangroves

The aerial, or above-ground, roots of mangrove plants trap muddy sediment to form wetland swamps. The Kinabatangan mangroves feature a range of lowland forests and open reed marsh.

**LOCATION**  Eastern Sabah, Malaysia

**TYPE**  Mangrove swamps

**SIZE**  400 sq miles (1,000 sq km)

## Yangtze estuary

The longest river in Asia and its busiest waterway, the Yangtze River carries large amounts of silt and mud, which are deposited in its estuary, dividing the river into three smaller channels and many streams.

**LOCATION**  Northwest Shanghai, China

**TYPE**  Estuary

**SIZE**  1,000 sq miles (2,500 sq km)

## Ha Long Bay

Rising sea levels flooded an area surrounding about 2,000 karst towers, creating the karst islands that make up Ha Long Bay. Some of these islands rise to about about 650 ft (200 m) above sea level.

**LOCATION**  Gulf of Tonkin, east Hanoi, Vietnam

**TYPE**  Land-based coast

**SIZE**  75 miles (120 km)

## Moeraki Beach

Moeraki Beach is famous for its large, round boulders, which are up to 10 ft (3 m) in diameter and can weigh several tons. The boulders formed as nodules in muddy sediment as it hardened into mudstone rock. The relatively soft mudstone has been worn away, leaving behind the harder boulders, which now litter the beach.

**LOCATION**  Northeast Dunedin, New Zealand

**TYPE**  Beach

**SIZE**  5 miles (8 km)

## Ninety Mile Beach

Made up of a series of sand dunes, this is the longest natural beach in the world. Behind these dunes lie several large lakes and shallow lagoons, known as the Gippsland Lakes.

**LOCATION**  Southwest Melbourne, Victoria, Australia

**TYPE**  Beach

**SIZE**  94 miles (150 km)

# The Twelve Apostles

When the roof of a natural rock arch erodes or collapses, it leaves behind a rock pillar called a stack. The Twelve Apostles is a group of sea stacks that were formed by the continuing wave erosion and collapse of 20-million-year-old limestone cliffs. They are still being eroded today.

**LOCATION** Near Port Campbell, Victoria, Australia

**TYPE** Marine-based coast

**SIZE** 2 miles (3 km)

These sea stacks are still called the Twelve Apostles, even though only eight of them remain today.

## SKELETON SHIPWRECKS

On the Skeleton Coast, cold air from the Atlantic Ocean and dry air from the Namib Desert form thick fogs, which have often caused sailors to lose their way. Many shipwrecks have been found here, including the *Eduard Bohlen*, which was washed ashore in 1909.

The Skeleton Coast is called

# "the land God made in anger,"

because of its harsh climate and dense ocean fog that has caused many shipwrecks

# Atmosphere

A layer of gases, called the atmosphere, surrounds the Earth. The Sun's rays pass through the atmosphere, warming the Earth's surface and the air above it, causing the air to move and water to evaporate. This results in different weather conditions. Changes in weather can also be caused by land-based events, such as the volcanic eruptions at Eyjafjallajökull, Iceland, in 2010, which created a huge ash cloud.

**DESTRUCTIVE WHIRL**
Swirling winds over warm ocean waters lead to hurricanes. In 2011, Hurricane Irene hit the US, the Atlantic coast of Canada, and the Caribbean.

# The Earth's atmosphere

The Earth is surrounded by a blanket of gases called the atmosphere, which is made up mainly of nitrogen and oxygen with tiny amounts of water vapor and other gases. The atmosphere is at its most dense near the Earth's surface. As altitude increases, it gets thinner, eventually fading into space.

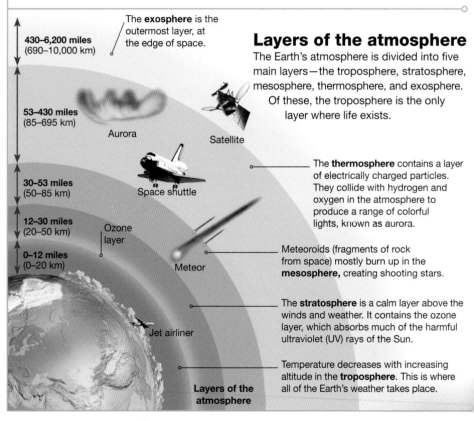

The **exosphere** is the outermost layer, at the edge of space.

430–6,200 miles (690–10,000 km)

53–430 miles (85–695 km)

Aurora

Satellite

30–53 miles (50–85 km)

Space shuttle

12–30 miles (20–50 km)

Ozone layer

0–12 miles (0–20 km)

Meteor

Jet airliner

**Layers of the atmosphere**

## Layers of the atmosphere

The Earth's atmosphere is divided into five main layers—the troposphere, stratosphere, mesosphere, thermosphere, and exosphere. Of these, the troposphere is the only layer where life exists.

The **thermosphere** contains a layer of electrically charged particles. They collide with hydrogen and oxygen in the atmosphere to produce a range of colorful lights, known as aurora.

Meteoroids (fragments of rock from space) mostly burn up in the **mesosphere,** creating shooting stars.

The **stratosphere** is a calm layer above the winds and weather. It contains the ozone layer, which absorbs much of the harmful ultraviolet (UV) rays of the Sun.

Temperature decreases with increasing altitude in the **troposphere**. This is where all of the Earth's weather takes place.

# Water and the atmosphere

The movement of water between the atmosphere, the land, and the Earth's oceans, lakes, and rivers is called the water cycle. The Sun's heat causes the Earth's liquid water to evaporate, or turn into water vapor. This water vapor rises and collects to form clouds. Water falls back to land and eventually returns to the oceans and lakes.

Clouds carry water to land in the form of **rain and snow**

Water **evaporates** from sea

Vapor cools to form **clouds**

Water seeps into **ground**

Water returns to sea via **rivers and streams**

**Water cycle**

# Jet streams

Jet streams are long, narrow bands of high-speed winds in the upper troposphere or lower stratosphere. The wind here is so strong that pilots can cut hours off their flight time by flying along these jet streams. Hot air from the aircraft engines condenses to form long, thin clouds of water vapor, known as contrails.

**Contrails above the Red Sea**

# Precipitation

When air cools, water vapor condenses—turns from gas into liquid—forming clouds. When cloud particles become too heavy to remain suspended in the air, they fall to the Earth as precipitation. This may be in the form of rain, snow, dew, fog, or hail.

## Dew

Dew forms overnight when warm, moist air rising from the ground meets cold night air, causing the rising moisture to condense on the ground as droplets of water.

**CLOUD** None
**INTENSITY** Light to heavy

## Rain

Rain is liquid precipitation that falls in drops. These vary in size from tiny drizzle as small as $^1/_{50}$ in ($^1/_2$ mm) wide to drops up to $^1/_4$ in (6 mm) wide. Most raindrops are $^2/_{25}$–$^1/_5$ in (2–5 mm) in diameter.

**CLOUD** Nimbostratus–cumulonimbus
**INTENSITY** Light to heavy

## Haar

Sea fog, or haar, is formed when warm moist air comes into contact with cold sea water and the moisture condenses into tiny droplets.

**CLOUD**  Low-level stratus

**INTENSITY**  Light to dense

## Hail

Hailstones are lumps of ice that form when frozen drops of rain, kept in the air by strong winds, get blown around in freezing thunderclouds until they are heavy enough to fall to the Earth. They may be smaller than peas or as big as oranges.

**CLOUD**  Tall cumulus

**INTENSITY**
Light to heavy

## Snow

When tiny ice crystals in clouds stick together, they form snowflakes. When they become heavy enough, they fall to the ground as snow. Snowfall is heaviest when temperatures are around freezing point, which is 32° F (0° C).

**CLOUD**  Cumulus and stratus

**INTENSITY**  Light to heavy

# Cloud types

Clouds consist of ice crystals or water droplets. According to the height of their base above the ground, they are identified as high, middle, or low. Cloud types are defined by air temperature and the amount of water in the cloud.

FOCUS ON...
## LIGHTNING
Electrical charges within clouds build up and result in lightning, seen in various shapes and forms in the sky.

## Cirrus

High, wispy clouds shaped like long streamers are called cirrus clouds or horse tails. These clouds are made up of ice crystals because they form in extremely cold parts of the atmosphere. Cirrus clouds are a sign of fair and pleasant weather.

**ALTITUDE**  18,000–40,000 ft (5,500–12,000 m)

**SHAPE**  Layered, tufted, or patchy

**PRECIPITATION**  None

## Cirrocumulus

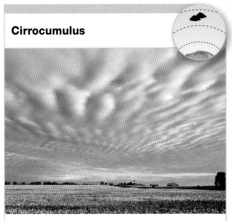

These rounded, white puffs are usually seen in long rows. They have ripples that resemble a honeycomb or the scales of a fish. Usually seen in the winter, they indicate fair but cold weather.

**ALTITUDE**  20,000–40,000 ft (6,000–12,000 m)

**SHAPE**  Layers or patches of cells

**PRECIPITATION**  None

▲ Cloud-to-ground lightning strikes the ground from a cumulonimbus cloud.

▲ Ground-to-cloud lightning moves from the ground to a cumulonimbus cloud.

▲ Cloud-to-cloud lightning occurs between different clouds, without touching the ground.

▲ Ball lightning is a bright ball that may occur with cloud-to-ground lightning.

## Cirrostratus

These thin, high, sheetlike clouds cover the entire sky, making it look milky. They are not thick enough to hide the Sun and Moon completely, but can produce a halo around them. They usually form 12–24 hours before a rain or snow storm.

**ALTITUDE**  18,000–40,000 ft (5,500–12,000 m)

**SHAPE**  Layered

**PRECIPITATION**  None

## Altocumulus

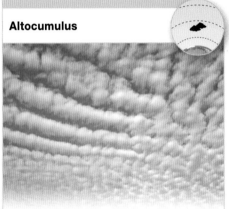

Altocumulus clouds look like rolls. These may be arranged in lines, waves, or round masses. If spotted on a warm, sticky morning, these clouds may indicate a thunderstorm will arrive late in the afternoon.

**ALTITUDE**  6,500–18,000 ft (2,000–5,500 m)

**SHAPE**  Parallel bands or rounded masses

**PRECIPITATION**  Possible thunderstorms or showers

## Altostratus

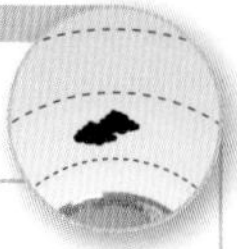

These clouds contain ice crystals near the top and water droplets lower down. Altostratus clouds can cover the entire sky in such a way that the Sun and Moon are faintly visible through them. These clouds may produce light snow or rain.

**ALTITUDE** 6,500–18,000 ft (2,000–5,500 m)

**SHAPE** Layered and featureless

**PRECIPITATION** Almost none

## Stratocumulus

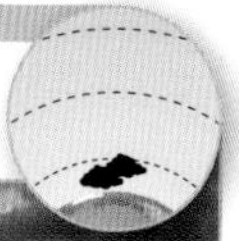

These low, puffy gray or white clouds are seen in rows, lines, or waves separated by patches of blue sky. They may appear in many weather conditions and can produce light rain or snow.

**ALTITUDE** 1,150–6,500 ft (350–2,000 m)

**SHAPE** Large and rounded

**PRECIPITATION** Light

## Stratus

Mostly featureless, these uniform gray or white clouds cover the sky in a blanket. They can form a layer thick enough to completely block out the Sun or Moon. They often form overnight in fine weather, especially over the sea.

**ALTITUDE** 0–6,500 ft (0–2,000 m)

**SHAPE** Layered

**PRECIPITATION** Light

## Cumulus

These individual, puffy clouds look like cotton balls floating in the sky. Cumulus clouds are flat at the base and have rounded tops that often look like cauliflower heads. They appear very white, with clearly defined edges.

**ALTITUDE** 0–6,500 ft (0–2,000 m)

**SHAPE** Cauliflower or fluffy

**PRECIPITATION** Occasional rain or snow showers

## Cumulonimbus

When cumulus clouds grow taller, they form giant cumulonimbus clouds. High winds flatten the tops of these thunderstorm clouds into the shape of an anvil, which points in the direction the storm is moving. These clouds produce heavy rain or snow, as well as hailstorms and tornadoes.

| | |
|---|---|
| **ALTITUDE** | 1,000–6,500 ft (300–2,000 m) |
| **SHAPE** | Stringy upper edges and anvil top |
| **PRECIPITATION** | Heavy rain and thunderstorms |

## Nimbostratus

## Lenticular clouds

These disk-shaped clouds form when the wind blows from the same direction at different levels of the troposphere. Usually seen in mountains or hilly areas, lenticular clouds are sometimes described as a "stack of pancakes."

**ALTITUDE**  6,500–16,400 ft (2,000–5,000 m)

**SHAPE**  Lens-shaped or saucerlike

**PRECIPITATION**  Possible light rain or snow

When altostratus clouds thicken, they develop into nimbostratus clouds. These are shapeless and dark, but may appear lit up from inside because of gaps in them. These clouds are so thick, they can hide the Sun and the Moon completely, resulting in dull days and dark nights.

**ALTITUDE**  2,000–10,000 ft (600–3,000 m)

**SHAPE**  Layered and featureless

**PRECIPITATION**  Continuous rain or snow likely

In 1959, William Rankin, a US Air Force pilot, had to eject from his burning aircraft and became the first person to survive a fall through a cumulonimbus cloud, after being **trapped inside it** for half an hour due to upward air currents

**CLOUDS OF DANGER**
Unlike other clouds, cumulonimbus clouds may release all their moisture at once, resulting in lightning, severe hailstorms, thunderstorms, and even tornadoes. This makes these clouds especially dangerous for planes to fly through.

# Storms

A storm is a powerful disturbance in the atmosphere. It typically features strong winds, cloudy skies, and heavy precipitation. Violent storms produce strong, fast winds such as tornadoes (narrow funnels of rapidly spinning air), cyclones (warm winds rising in a spiral), and hurricanes (tropical cyclones).

## Storm of the Century

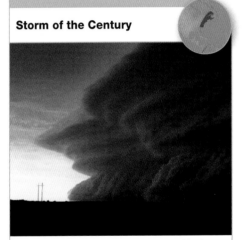

This week-long storm was accompanied by heavy snow, tornadoes, and freezing temperatures. Severe snowstorms, called blizzards, caused major damage to power lines, leading to power failures that affected more than 10 million people.

**LOCATION**  US and Canada
**YEAR**  1993
**TYPE**  Snowstorm

## Oklahoma Tornado Outbreak

Situated in a tornado-prone area, the state of Oklahoma experiences several hundred tornadoes every year. On May 3, 1999, more than 70 tornadoes struck the state, causing widespread destruction—demolishing thousands of homes and whipping up huge clouds of debris. The storms lasted for three days and caused damage worth a billion dollars.

**LOCATION**  Oklahoma
**YEAR**  1999
**TYPE**  Tornado

## Hurricane Katrina

One of the five deadliest hurricanes to hit the US, Hurricane Katrina killed more than 1,800 people and caused damage worth 90 billion dollars. In New Orleans, high waves and torrential rains led to widespread flooding. About 80 percent of the city was flooded up to a depth of 23 ft (7 m).

**LOCATION**  New Orleans, Louisiana

**YEAR**  2005

**TYPE**  Cyclone

## Great Ice Storm

A combination of five smaller ice storms, this storm resulted in more than 80 hours of freezing rain. Layers of ice built up, damaging trees and bringing down power lines. This caused massive power failures, with some areas remaining without power for weeks.

**LOCATION**  Canada and US

**YEAR**  1998

**TYPE**  Ice storm

## Cyclone Nargis

The deadliest cyclone ever recorded in this region, Nargis caused massive damage and many deaths, both during the storm and after it ended. Several thousand people drowned, while others died of diseases caused by rotting bodies, dirty floodwater, and mosquitoes.

| | |
|---|---|
| **LOCATION** | Myanmar |
| **YEAR** | 2008 |
| **TYPE** | Cyclone |

## Chinese Dust Storm

Dust and sand storms occur in arid or semiarid areas where there aren't enough trees to hold the soil in place and it gets whipped up into the air by the wind. This dust storm from the Gobi Desert covered 313,000 sq miles (810,000 sq km).

| | |
|---|---|
| **LOCATION** | China |
| **YEAR** | 2010 |
| **TYPE** | Dust storm |

## Red Dust Storm

A cloud of red-orange dust, more than 600 miles (1,000 km) long, spread from Australia's deserts and dry farmland to Sydney and the eastern coast of Australia. This storm caused major disruption to international flights.

| | |
|---|---|
| **LOCATION** | Eastern coast of Australia |
| **YEAR** | 2009 |
| **TYPE** | Dust storm |

## Black Saturday Bushfires

The heat from the wildfire was powerful enough to kill anyone within 1,000 ft (300 m).

When lightning strikes dry vegetation, it can cause a fire. This wildfire started as nine small fires. High-speed winds of up to 56 mph (90 kph) rapidly spread the fires, causing massive damage.

**LOCATION** Victoria, Australia

**YEAR** 2009

**TYPE** Wildfire

In 1931, a powerful tornado in Mississippi

# lifted a train

weighing 91 tons (83 metric tonnes) up into the air and tossed it 80 ft (24 m) away from the track

**TORNADO FORCE**
A tornado, or twister, is a storm in which a column of air, usually about 328 ft (100 m) wide, spins violently. It can completely destroy an area, uprooting trees, overturning cars, and wrecking buildings.

# Climate

The weather changes every day, with variations in temperature, precipitation, wind, and clouds. When the weather is examined over several years, a pattern emerges. This pattern, repeated over many years, is known as the climate of a particular region. Scientists divide the world into regions according to their climates. These regions range from icy polar zones to hot tropical areas.

**GLOBAL WARMING**
At present, the average global temperature is rising, but this rise is not spread evenly around the Earth. Some areas are getting warmer, while others are getting colder.

# Global warming

Global warming is the term given to the rise in the Earth's average temperature. Climate change is a natural process and has been going on for billions of years. However, human activity has recently caused the rate of change to increase, which is causing many serious environmental problems.

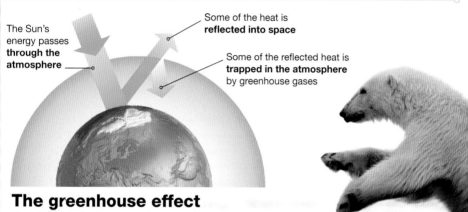

The Sun's energy passes **through the atmosphere**

Some of the heat is **reflected into space**

Some of the reflected heat is **trapped in the atmosphere** by greenhouse gases

## The greenhouse effect

Certain gases in the atmosphere trap heat that would otherwise escape back into space. This is known as the greenhouse effect. The gases that cause it—carbon dioxide, methane, and water vapor—are called greenhouse gases.

## Causes of global warming

Greenhouse gases, which increase the greenhouse effect, are released into the atmosphere by aircraft and car exhausts, as well as when fossil fuels are burned in factories and power plants. Greenhouse gases are also found in aerosols and old refrigerators.

## Effects of global warming

Aside from changing weather patterns and frequent storms, the high rate of global warming causes glaciers and polar ice to melt. This may lead to a rise in sea levels, flooding low-lying areas. This can threaten plants and animals that may not be able to adapt quickly enough to the change, such as polar bears. Ice is vital for them— they use it as a bridge to move across the ocean to hunt for food. If this ice melts, these bears may not survive.

## Helping the planet

To try to stop global warming, the release of greenhouse gases into the atmosphere from factories, cars, and other sources will have to be reduced. The use of "cleaner," renewable energy sources, such as solar and wind power, will help, as will the recycling of materials (such as paper), environmentally friendly transportation (such as cycling), and the replanting of forests.

# Climate regions

The climate of a region determines its main characteristics—temperature, rainfall, soil type, and plant growth. Based on these, regions are identified and classified into different biomes, or climate regions.

## Temperate

Temperate areas have varied climates, but the average monthly temperature ranges between 64°F (18°C) and 27°F (-3°C). In the warmest month, the average temperature is above 50°F (10°C). These regions have four distinct seasons, but can experience unpredictable weather throughout the year.

**DISTRIBUTION**   Most regions lying between the tropical and polar regions

**TYPICAL LOCATION**   Cork, Ireland, where temperature ranges from 48°F (9°C) to 68°F (20°C)

## Tropical

Humid, tropical climates have a high annual rainfall and an average yearly temperature of at least 64°F (18°C). More than half the world's species of plant are found in these regions, which typically feature a dense tree cover.

▲ Areas close to the equator are hotter as the Sun's rays fall directly on these regions.

▲ Oceans absorb and transport heat from the Sun, giving coastal regions a moderate climate.

▲ Temperature decreases at higher altitudes, making mountains colder than lower-lying areas.

**DISTRIBUTION** Most regions along the equator

**TYPICAL LOCATION** Dodoma, Tanzania, where temperature ranges from 79°F (26°C) to 88°F (31°C)

## Mountain

Although temperature decreases with height everywhere, the climate of each mountain varies according to the region in which it is located. For example, those parts of the Andes that lie in Colombia receive frequent rainfall, but parts that lie in Ecuador are usually dry.

**DISTRIBUTION** Mountains, plateaus, and ranges, about 2,000 ft (600 m) above sea level

**TYPICAL LOCATION** Les Escaldes, Andorra, where temperature ranges from 43°F (6°C) to 79°F (26°C)

# Polar

The Arctic and Antarctic regions, located at the Earth's North and South poles, have an extremely cold and dry climate. All precipitation falls as snow, which remains on the ground and builds up gradually over time.

**DISTRIBUTION** Arctic and Antarctic circles

**TYPICAL LOCATION** Vostok Station, Antarctica, where the temperature ranges from -89°F (-67°C) to -26°F (-32°C)

# Mediterranean

Regions with mild, wet winters and warm, dry summers are said to have a Mediterranean climate. Rainfall averages 15 in (380 mm) a year, falling mainly between December and March, with usually no rain at all in August.

**DISTRIBUTION** Southern Europe, South Africa, and southern Australia

**TYPICAL LOCATION** Rome, Italy, where the temperature ranges from 52°F (11°C) to 86°F (30°C)

# Arid

Arid areas are hot and dry, with high levels of evaporation and low precipitation. They include hot deserts such as the Sahara, which receives no rain for years, and semidesert areas such as the Sahel, which has a short rainy season.

**DISTRIBUTION**  Most deserts

**TYPICAL LOCATION**  I-n-Salah, Algeria, where the temperature ranges from 70°F (21°C) to 113°F (45°C).

# Did you know?

## EARTH STATISTICS

★ The Earth is **4.6 billion years old.**

★ The first appearance of life on the Earth occurred at least **3.4 billion years ago,** as shown by fossils of microbes found in Australia.

★ The Earth's diameter at the equator is **7,926 miles (12,756 km).**

★ The Earth measures **24,900 miles (40,075 km)** around the equator.

★ The average distance of the Earth from the Sun is **93 million miles (149.6 million km).**

★ The average distance that the Earth's tectonic plates move in one year is **4½ in (11 cm).**

★ The depth of the troposphere varies between **5 and 11 miles (8 and 18 km).**

★ The Earth orbits the Sun at a speed of **67,000 mph (107,300 kph).**

★ The Earth rotates at **994 mph (1,600 kph),** completing one spin every 24 hours.

★ The Earth spins on an axis that is at present tilted **23.5°** from the vertical. This tilt means that different amounts of sunlight reach the Earth's surface as it orbits the Sun over a year, resulting in the seasons.

★ It takes **8.3 minutes** for light from the Sun to reach the Earth.

★ The Earth's average surface temperature is **59°F (15°C).**

## DISCOVERY AND INVENTION

The following are some of the most important Earth-related scientific discoveries and inventions from the past few thousand years.

▶ **c.280** BCE
Greek astronomer Aristarchus is the first to estimate the **distance between the Earth and the Sun.** He also suggests that the planet Earth rotates on its axis and revolves around the Sun, although few people believe him at this time.

▶ **23** CE
Greek geographer and historian Strabo states that **earthquakes and volcanoes** cause land to rise and sink.

▶ **c.1100**
The Chinese invent the **magnetic compass.**
It uses a pivoting magnetized needle to point
to the Earth's poles.

▶ **1519–21**
Portuguese navigator Ferdinand Magellan
sets out on the **first sailing expedition
around the world.** He is killed in the
Philippines, but the surviving sailors
complete the voyage.

▶ **1543**
Polish astronomer Nicolaus Copernicus
argues that the **planets orbit the Sun
and that the Earth spins on its axis.**
Until this time, most people believed that the
Earth lay at the center of the universe.

▶ **1609**
Italian astronomer and mathematician
Galileo Galilei uses a telescope to produce
the first scientific proof for Copernicus's theory
about the **movement of the planets.**

▶ **1669**
Danish scholar Nicolaus Steno describes
the **principles of stratigraphy.** This says
that layers of rock, or strata, are deposited
one on top of the other, with the youngest
strata being on top.

▶ **1798**
English physicist Henry Cavendish determines
the **mass and density** of the Earth.

▶ **1824**
William Buckland of the University of Oxford
writes the **first scientific paper about a
dinosaur,** pioneering the use of fossils to
reconstruct the Earth's timeline.

▶ **1827**
French mathematician Jean Baptiste
Fourier introduces the concept of the
**greenhouse effect.**

▶ **1880**
English geologist John Milne invents the
**modern seismograph** (an instrument
for measuring earthquakes).

▶ **1895**
Swedish chemist Svante Arrhenius
suggests that carbon dioxide added to the
Earth's atmosphere helps trap heat from
the Sun, leading to **global warming.**

▶ **1912**
German meteorologist Alfred Wegener
proposes the theory of **continental drift.**
He claims that about 270 mya a giant
landmass, the supercontinent of Pangaea,
broke up into smaller pieces, leading to the
continents we recognize today.

▶ **1953**
US scientist Claire Patterson first
accurately **estimates the Earth's age**
by comparing measurements taken
from meteorites and minerals.

# Amazing Earth facts

## HIGHEST MOUNTAINS

**❶ Mount Everest,** in the Himalayas, is the Earth's highest mountain, at 29,035 ft (8,850 m) above sea level.

**❷ K2** is part of the northwestern region of the Karakoram Range. This peak stands at a height of 28,250 ft (8,611 m) above sea level.

**❸ Kanchenjunga** means "the five treasures of snows." It is named for its five peaks, of which the highest is 28,169 ft (8,586 m) above sea level.

**❹ Lhotse** is 27,940 ft (8,516 m) above sea level. It is found on the border between Tibet and the Khumbu region of Nepal.

**❺ Makalu,** in the Himalayas, is an isolated peak shaped like a four-sided pyramid. It is 27,766 ft (8,463 m) high.

**❻ Cho Oyu** is 26,906 ft (8,201 m) above sea level. It lies in the Himalayas and is 12²/₅ miles (20 km) west of Mount Everest, on the border between China and Nepal.

**❼ Dhaulagiri** is 26,795 ft (8,167 m) high. Its name means "pure white mountain."

**❽ Manaslu** is 26,781 ft (8,163 m) above sea level and is a part of the Nepalese Himalayas, in the west-central part of Nepal. Manaslu is also known as Kutang.

**❾ Nanga Parbat** is known in Kashmir, India, as Diamir, which means "king of the mountains." It rises to a height of 26,657 ft (8,125 m).

**❿ Annapurna** is a section of the Himalayas in north-central Nepal. Its highest peak is 26,542 ft (8,090 m) high.

Measured from its oceanic base, Mauna Kea in Hawaii is more than 33,465 ft (10,200 m) high—even taller than Mount Everest.

## DEADLIEST ERUPTIONS

**❶** In 1815, the **Tambora volcano** erupted in Indonesia, sending dust clouds around the globe and dimming the sun. Around 70,000 people were killed from the eruption and its after effects, such as famine and disease.

**❷** The **Krakatau volcano** exploded in 1883, killing around 36,000 people. This explosion is believed to be the loudest sound recorded in recent history.

❸ In 1902, the town of St. Pierre, on the Caribbean island of Martinique, was destroyed by burning clouds of dust from **Mount Pelée.** This eruption killed more than 29,000 people.

❹ In 1985, the eruption of the **Ruiz volcano,** in Colombia, caused a massive mudflow, which engulfed the town of Armero, 37 miles (60 km) away. More than 25,000 people were buried in the mud.

❺ **Mount Unzen** is an active group of several overlapping stratovolcanoes in Japan. In 1792, the collapse of one of its lava domes triggered a tsunami that killed about 15,000 people.

❻ In 1783, **Laki Mountain,** in Iceland, poured out lava and gases, which spread as far as Europe and North America. Around 9,500 people were killed in Iceland alone.

❼ The eruption of **Santa Maria** in Guatemala, in 1902, was one of the largest volcanic eruptions of the 20th century. Around 6,000 people were killed.

❽ **Kelud,** a volcano in Indonesia, is known for large, explosive eruptions. More than 30 eruptions have occurred since 1000 CE. In 1919, an eruption at Kelud killed an estimated 5,000 people.

❾ **Galunggung** is an active stratovolcano in west Java, Indonesia. In 1822, an eruption killed more than 4,000 people.

❿ **Mount Vesuvius** is a stratovolcano in the Gulf of Naples, Italy. Since the famous eruption of 79 CE, which destroyed the city of Pompeii and the town of Herculaneum, it has erupted many times.

# DEEPEST OCEANIC TRENCHES

❶ At a depth of 35,794 ft (10,910 m), the **Mariana Trench** in the Pacific Ocean is the deepest spot in the world's oceans.

❷ Located in the southern Pacific Ocean, the **Tonga Trench** is up to 35,700 ft (10,880 m) deep.

❸ The **Kuril–Kamchatka Trench** or Kuril Trench is located in the northwestern part of the Pacific Ocean. It is 34,587 ft (10,542 m) deep.

❹ The **Philippines Trench** is a submarine trench that lies to the east of the Philippines. It is 34,580 ft (10,540 m) deep.

❺ The **Kermadec Trench,** which is 32,972 ft (10,050 m) deep, was formed by the subduction of the Pacific Plate under the Indo-Australian Plate.

# Glossary

**Algae** A diverse group of simple plantlike organisms, the largest of which are seaweeds.

**Arid** A weather condition that is very dry and supports little plant and animal life.

**Aurora** Bands of colored light in the sky over the North and South poles.

**Basaltic lava** The hottest type of lava, with the lowest silica content. It is runnier than other lavas and cools to form basalt.

**Basin** A depression on the Earth's surface filled with water, from where a river and all its branches and tributaries drain.

**Batholith** A huge mass of igneous rock that often forms the core of mountains.

**Beach** An area of land marking the margin of a coastline. It usually consists of loose rock particles, such as sand, gravel, or pebbles.

**Biome** A region of the Earth that has a particular type of climate, soil, and plant and animal life.

**Blizzard** A storm in which thick snow falls fast and hard.

**Boreal** An ecosystem or habitat of or related to sub-Arctic areas, usually used to describe forests of that region.

**Caldera** A crater, or depression, at the top of a volcano. It forms when the peak collapses into the volcano's magma chamber.

**Condensation** The change of water vapor into liquid water.

**Coniferous forest** A biome that is made up of coniferous trees. It has cold, snowy winters and warm, humid summers.

**Cyclone** A storm in which warm, moist winds rise in a spiral. A tropical cyclone is also called a hurricane.

**Delta** The sediment deposited at the mouth of a river. It usually forms a triangular shape.

**Drizzle** Small droplets of liquid precipitation, formed in a low-layer cloud.

**Dyke** A thin, sheetlike body of igneous rock that cuts into older rocks.

**Environment** The physical features of an area, including air, water, and soil.

**Equator** An imaginary line around the middle of the Earth. It is at an equal distance from both poles.

**Erosion** The wearing away and transportation of soil and rock by wind, gravity, water, or ice.

**Estuary** A type of wetland where fresh water mixes with seawater at the mouth of a river.

**Evaporation** The change of liquid water into water vapor.

**Fjord** A valley that has been deepened by a glacier and then filled with seawater.

**Fog** A thick cloud that forms at or near the Earth's surface.

**Fossil** The remains or impression of an organism preserved in rock.

**Fossil fuel** A carbon compound, such as coal or natural gas, formed over millions of years, from the compressed, decayed remains of dead organisms. It is burned to release energy.

**Fumarole** A volcanic vent or opening that emits gases.

**Geyser** A spring that releases boiling water and steam from the ground. It is formed when ground water is heated up by magma inside the Earth.

**Gorge** A narrow, deep valley, usually with vertical cliffs on each side.

**Ground water** Underground water, held in gaps in soil or rocks.

**Habitat** The environment in which an organism lives.

**Hemisphere** The term used to describe the northern and southern halves of the Earth as divided by the equator.

**Hurricane** A powerful storm that blows over tropical oceans. In many parts of the world, a hurricane is known as a typhoon or cyclone.

**Icecap** A mass of permanent ice covering a large area, especially in polar regions.

**Ice sheet** A layer of permanent ice covering a vast area of land.

**Ice shelf** An ice sheet extending into the ocean.

**Karst** A landscape formed by the dissolving of rock, usually limestone, by water. Karsts often feature large networks of caves.

**Lagoon** An area of shallow sea that is separated from the main sea by sand or a reef.

**Lava** Molten rock that has erupted onto the surface of the Earth from deep within the crust.

**Lightning** A discharge of electricity in the sky.

**Magma** Molten rock formed deep within the Earth.

**Magma chamber** An area beneath a volcano where magma builds up before an eruption.

**Marsh** A type of low-lying wetland that is typically covered with grass and reeds.

**Midocean ridge** An underwater volcanic mountain range formed where tectonic plates part and lava erupts through the gap to form a new ocean floor.

**Migration** A regular journey, usually seasonal, made by an animal in search of food, water, or good breeding conditions.

**Mineral** A natural chemical substance that makes up rocks.

**Orbit** The path on which a planet travels around the Sun, or a moon travels around a planet.

**Organic** Anything that is living or has been formed by a living organism.

**Peninsula** A body of land that is surrounded by water on three sides.

**Permafrost** Soil that remains frozen for at least two years. It occurs mainly in polar regions.

**Plankton** Tiny living organisms that float or drift near the surface of the sea.

**Plateau** A large area of flat land that stands above its surroundings.

**Rift** A widening, valleylike crack in the Earth's crust.

**Salinity** The saltiness of a substance—for example, water.

**Savanna** An area of grassland with very few trees that occurs at the edge of the tropics.

**Sediments** Particles of rock, mineral, or organic matter that are carried by wind, water, and ice. The deposition of these particles is called sedimentation.

**Sill** An igneous rock formation that occurs as a flat layer. It is formed when magma is squeezed between layers of existing rocks.

**Stalactite** An icicle-shaped mineral deposit that hangs from the roof of a cave.

**Stalagmite** An icicle-shaped mineral deposit that builds up from the floor of a cave.

**Storm** A violent disturbance in the Earth's atmosphere. It is usually accompanied by strong winds and heavy precipitation.

**Subduction** The term used to describe the movement of one tectonic plate beneath another. Subduction often occurs at convergent boundaries.

**Supercontinent** An enormous landmass consisting of several continental plates.

**Temperate** Of or relating to biomes with cool, varied climate throughout the year.

**Temperature** The degree or intensity of heat present in an object or organism.

**Thunder** The sound produced by the instant, intense heating and expansion of air by lightning.

**Tornado** A violent and destructive storm with a funnel cloud and strong, spinning winds.

**Tropical** Of or relating to biomes that have a hot, humid climate with plenty of rainfall.

**Tsunami** A massive, often destructive wave, caused by earthquakes or volcanic eruptions.

**Ultraviolet (UV) rays** Certain rays of the Sun that can be harmful.

**Volcanic plug** A core of solidified molten rock that blocks the neck of a volcano.

**Volcano** A vent in the Earth's crust through which magma erupts, as well as the structure created by this eruption.

**Water vapor** The gaseous form of water.

# Index

# Acknowledgments

Dorling Kindersley would like to thank:
Caitlin Doyle for proofreading and Helen Peters
for indexing.

The publisher would like to thank the following
for their kind permission to reproduce
their photographs:

(Key: a-above; b-below/bottom; c-center; f-far; l-left;
r-right; t-top)

1 NASA: Visible Earth / Reto Stockli / Alan Nelson /
Fritz Hasler (clb). 2–3 Getty Images: Ron Dahlquist /
Perspectives (c). 4–5 Science Photo Library: Mark
Garlick (b). 5 Dreamstime.com: Brett Critchley (crb).
NASA: Visible Earth / Reto Stockli / Alan Nelson / Fritz
Hasler (tr / Earth); JPL (tc, tl, tl / Uranus, tc / Mars, tr /
Venus); Hubble Space Telescope Collection (tr, tr /
Mercury, tc / Jupiter). 6 Corbis: Reg Morrison / Auscape
/ Minden Pictures (cl). 6–7 Dorling Kindersley: Peter
Minister, Digital Sculptor (tc). 7 Getty Images:
Encyclopaedia Britannica / UIG (cr); Max Dannenbaum /
Stone (br). 8–9 Dorling Kindersley: Satellite Imagemap
Copyright (c) 1996–2003 Planetary Visions (c). 9
Dreamstime.com: Keith Wheatley (br). Shutterstock:
(cr). 12 Corbis: Lloyd Cluff (b). 13 Corbis: Xinhua /
XINHUA (tr). NASA: (cb); JSC Digital Image Collection
(bl). 14–15 Getty Images: Carsten Peter / Speleoresearch
and Films / National Geographic. 16 Corbis: George
Steinmetz. 17 Getty Images: Sami Sarkis /
Photographer's Choice RF (bc). 18 Dreamstime.com:
Yarek Gora (cr); Stephan Pietzko (c). 19 Courtesy of
the National Science Foundation: Peter Rejcek (tl).
Shutterstock: (cra, bc). 20 Dreamstime.com: Mike
Brake (bl); Steve Estvanik (br). 21 Corbis: Momatiuk-
Eastcott (tr). Dreamstime.com: Sergeytoronto (b). 22
Dreamstime.com: Ams22 (tl). 22–23 Getty Images: Yann
Arthus-Bertrand (bc); Kay Nietfeld / dpa (tc). 23 Getty
Images: LatitudeStock / David Forman / Gallo Images
(br). 24 Corbis: Myung Jo Lee / Aflo Relax (t); Nigel
Pavitt / JAI (br). 25 Corbis: Galen Rowell (bl).
Dreamstime.com: Blagov58 (t). 26 Dreamstime.
com: Leonid Spektor (b). 26–27 Corbis: Roger
Ressmeyer (bc). 27 Alamy Images: FLPA (br). Corbis:
Richard Roscoe / Stocktrek Images (tl); Lothar Slabon /
Epa (tr). 28 Corbis: Vittoriano Rastelli (bl). 28–29
Corbis: Kazuyoshi Nomachi (c). 29 Corbis: George
Steinmetz (br). Dreamstime.com: Craig Hanson (b).
30–31 Corbis: Alberto Garcia. 32 Dreamstime.com:
Derekteo (b). 33 Corbis: Roger Ressmeyer (bl); Ralph
White (b). Dorling Kindersley: Natural History Museum,
London (b). Dreamstime.com: Adreslebedev (cl);
Miloslav Doubrava (br). 34 Dreamstime.com:
Dariophotography (cl). 34–35 Dreamstime.com:
Piter99 (tc). 35 Corbis: Yann Arthus-Bertrand (cr).
Dreamstime.com: Davedt (bl). 39 Alamy Images:
WidStock (tr). 41 Dreamstime.com: Victorua (br).
Getty Images: Olivier Goujon / Robert Harding World
Imagery (t). 42 Corbis: NASA (bl). 42–43 Dreamstime.
com: Ewamewa2 (bc). Getty Images: Robert Caputo /
Aurora (t). 43 Alamy Images: Bill Bachman (br). Corbis:
Martin Harvey. 44–45 Dreamstime.com: Chun
Guo. 46 Dreamstime.com: Giovanni Gagliardi (b).
46–47 Corbis: Adam Woolfitt (b). 47 Alamy Images:
Olivier Parent (t). Corbis: Frans Lanting (b). 48 Getty
Images: Marilyn Angel Wynn / Nativestock (bl); David
Prichard / First Light (br). 49 Corbis: Scott T. Smith (tl).

Dreamstime.com: Meandr (b). 50 Dreamstime.com:
Dshamanov (b). 50–51 Dreamstime.com: Alexandr
Malyshev (tc); Witr (bc). 51 Science Photo Library:
Marshall Space Flight Center / Nasa (br). 52 Corbis:
Sean Russell / fstop (b). 53 Alamy Images: Juergen
Richter (b). Getty Images: Randy Wells / Stone (tr). 54
Corbis: Kazuyoshi Nomachi (br). Dreamstime.com:
Lagartija (bl). Getty Images: Natphotos / Digital Vision
(t). 55 Alamy Images: Images and Stories (t). Getty
Images: Peter Walton Photography / Photolibrary (b).
56 NASA: (bl). 56–57 Dreamstime.com: Maxfx (tc).
Corbis: James Balog / Aurora Photos (bc). 57 Corbis:
Frank Krahmer (br). Dreamstime.com: Ihervas (cr).
58–59 Getty Images: moodboard / the Agency
Collection. 60 Alamy Images: Chris Mattison (cl).
Tony Waltham Geophotos: (b). 61 Getty Images:
Joe Cornish / The Image Bank (t). SuperStock:
imagebroker.net (br). Tony Waltham Geophotos: (clb).
62 Corbis: Momatiuk—Eastcott (bl). Dreamstime.com:
Attila Tatár (br). 63 Corbis: Peter Johnson (br).
Dreamstime.com: Genghiscat (tl). Getty Images: Cris
Bouroncle / Afp (tc); Danita Delimont / Gallo Images (tr);
Frans Lemmens / Stone (cl). 64 Corbis: Paul Souders
(t); George Steinmetz (b). 65 Getty Images: Ted Mead /
Photolibrary (tl, b). 66–67 Corbis: Ed Darack / Science
Faction. 68 Alamy Images: Arco Images / Meissner, D
(cr). Shutterstock: Yuriy Kulyk (cl). 69 Corbis: Jim
Brandenburg / Minden Pictures (cl); Jochen Schlenker /
Westend61 (cr); Frans Lanting (b). 70 Corbis: Adrian
Arbib (bl). Getty Images: Tim Graham (tr). 70–71
Dreamstime.com: Steffen Foerster (bc). 71 Corbis:
Frans Lanting (tr). 72 Corbis: Ocean. 73 Getty Images:
Ted Mead / Photolibrary (br); Peter Walton Photography /
Photolibrary (t). 74 Getty Images: DEA / P Jaccod (br);
Zack Seckler / The Image Bank (bl). 75 Corbis: Haiku
Expressed / First Light (t); ony Waltham / Robert
Harding World Imagery (br); Image Source (cl). 76
Corbis: Alaska Stock (b). 77 Corbis: Jenny E. Ross.
78–79 Getty Images: Robert Postma / First Light. 80
Alamy Images: Bill Bachman (cr). Dreamstime.com:
Bondarenko Olesya (b). 81 Dreamstime.com: Ina Van
Hateren (cl), Ivan Kok Cheong Hor (cr). Getty Images:
Peter Walton Photography / Photolibrary (b). 82 Corbis:
Danny Lehman (tr). Dreamstime.com: Saurabh13 (b).
83 Corbis: airyuhi / a.collectionRF / amanaimages (b);
Ocean (cr). Dreamstime.com: Lucaparodi (cl). 84
Getty Images: Matt Cardy. 85 Corbis: David Wrobel /
Visuals Unlimited (b). 87 NASA: (cr). 89 Corbis: Galen
Rowell (t); Paul Souders (br). Dreamstime.com: Oleg
Kozlov (bl). 90–91 Getty Images: Slow Images /
Photographer's Choice (bc). 91 Dreamstime.com: Patryk
Kosmider (t). Getty Images: Ron Erwin / All Canada
Photos (tr). 92 Corbis: Dave Reede / All Canada Photos
(bl). 92–93 Getty Images: Carlos Davila / Photographer's
Choice RF (bc). 94 Getty Images: Image Source (b).
95 Dreamstime.com: Mohamed Farhadi (b); Lestor
(tr). 96 Corbis: Michael S. Yamashita (br). 97 Dorling
Kindersley: Rough Guide (t). Dreamstime.com: Bin
Zhou (b). 98–99 Getty Images: Frank Krahmer / Riser
(b). 99 Getty Images: Fotosearch (tl); Wayne Lynch / All
Canada Photos (br). 100–101 Corbis: Frans Lanting.
102–103 Getty Images: Panoramic Images (b). 103
Dreamstime.com: Barefootflyer (tl, tr); Debra Law
(tc); Melvinlee (cl). 104 Alamy Images: Stephen Frink
Collection (tr). Dreamstime.com: Asther Lau Choon
Siew (cl); David Espin (tl); Harmonia101 (tr). 105
Corbis: Martin Harvey (tr); Kevin Schafer (bl). Getty

Images: Saki Ono / Flickr Open (br). 106 Corbis:
Carlos Villoch / Robert Harding Specialist Stock. 107
Alamy Images: Jeff Mondragon (tr). Getty Images:
Aaron Foster / Photographer's Choice (br). 108–109
Corbis: Vilainecrevette. 110 Alamy Images:
Clint Farlinger (br). Dreamstime.com: Sibel Aisha (tl);
David Woods (bl). 111 Corbis: Buddy Mays (cr); Neil
Rabinowitz (cl). Dreamstime.com: John.59 (b). 112
Corbis: Michele Falzone / JAI (b). Getty Images:
Thomas Dressler / Gallo Images (tr). 113 Corbis:
Thomas Marent / Minden Pictures (cl). Dreamstime.
com: Piotnikov (b). NASA: Visible Earth (cr). 114 Alamy
Images: Bill Bachman (tr). 115 Dreamstime.com:
Daria Angelova. 116–117 Getty Images: George Steinmetz.
118 Corbis: Arctic-Images. 119 NASA: Scientific
Visualization Studio Collection (bc). 120 NASA: (c, bc).
Courtesy of the National Science Foundation: Rhys
Boulton (cr). 121 Corbis: (br). 122 Corbis: Imaginechina
(bl); Frank Krahmer (tr). 123 Corbis: W. Perry Conway
(b). Getty Images: Don Johnston / All Canada Photos
(br); SuperStock (ca). 124 Corbis: Jim Craigmyle (cr).
Dreamstime.com: Rudy Umans (b). 125 Corbis: Mark
Laricchia (tc); Ocean (bl). Dreamstime.com: Ben
Goode (tc / Cloud-to-Cloud); Skydaver42 (tr); Intrepix
(cr). Getty Images: Stocktrek Images (tl). 126 Getty
Images: Graeme Norways / Stone (b). 127 Corbis:
Onne van der Wal (t). Dreamstime.com: William
Manning (b). 128–129 Corbis: Adam Jones / Visuals
Unlimited (c). 128 Dreamstime.com: Seus (b). 129
Corbis: Momatiuk—Eastcott (br). 130–131 Corbis:
Mike Hollingshead / Science Faction. 132 Douglas P.
Berry: (c). Corbis: Jim Reed (br). 133 Corbis:
Christopher J. Morris (b); Mike Theiss / Ultimate Chase
(t). 134 Dreamstime.com: Gordon Tipene (br). Getty
Images: STR / AFP (cr). NASA: Earth Observatory / Jeff
Schmaltz (tr). 135 Corbis: Andrew Brownbill / Epa.
136–137 Getty Images: Willoughby Owen / Flickr. 138
Corbis: Paul Souders. 139 Dreamstime.com: Ollirg
(bc). 140–141 Corbis: Paul Souders (b). 141 Corbis:
Liu Liqun (tl). Dreamstime.com: Aji Jayachandran (cr).
142 Getty Images: John W Banagan / Stockbyte (b).
142–143 Dreamstime.com: Asci advertising and
Publishing (bc). 144 Corbis: David DuChemin / Design
Pics (b); Colin Monteath / Hedgehog House / Minden
Pictures (t). 145 Corbis: George Steinmetz.

Jacket images: Front: Dorling Kindersley: Chris
Reynolds and the BBC Team, cb, Andy Crawford /
Donks Models—modelmaker, cr, David Donkin—
modelmaker, ftr, cl, Donks Models—modelmaker, tr,
crb, Donk Models—modelmaker, tc, Simon Mumford,
c. PunchStock: Photodisc, clb; Back: Dorling
Kindersley: Donks Models—modelmaker, clb;
Spine: Dorling Kindersley: Simon Mumford, t.

All other images © Dorling Kindersley

For further information see: www.dkimages.com